The Letters of Carla, the letter b.

A Mystery in Poetry

with a foreword by
The Future Guardian of the Letters

and an afterword by
Benjamin Hollander

chax

2017

Chax Press / PO Box 162 / Victoria, TX 77902-0162

Poem by Mahmoud Darwish, "Mural," which precedes the Foreword
to this book, is used with permission.

Chax Press is supported in part by the School of Arts & Sciences
at the University of Houston-Victoria. We are located in the UHV
Center for the Arts in downtown Victoria, Texas. We acknowledge
the support of graduate and undergraduate student interns and
assistants who contribute to the books we publish. In Fall 2016 and
Spring 2017 our interns are Julieta Woleslagle, Sophia Kameitjo,
Errin Maye, and Gabrielle Delao. This book is also supported by
private donors. We are thankful to all of our contributors and
members. Please see http://chax.org/support/ for more information.

Library of Congress Cataloging-in-Publication Data

Names: Hollander, Benjamin, author.
  Title: The letters of Carla, the letter b. : a mystery in poetry /
  Benjamin   Hollander ; with a foreword by the Future Guardian
  of the Letters ; and an afterword by Benjamin Hollander.
Description: Victoria, TX : Chax, 2017.
Identifiers: LCCN 2016051512l ISBN 9781946104014 (softcover
  acid-free paper) l ISBN 9781946104021 (hardcover : acid-free
  paper)
Classification: LCC PS3558.O34923 A6 2017 l DDC 811/.54--dc23
LC record available at https://lccn.loc.gov/2016051512

Contents

جداريَّة

هذا هُوَ آسمُكَ/

قالتِ آمرأةٌ،

وغابتْ في المَمَرّ اللولبيّ ...

أرى السماء هُناكَ في مُتَناوَلِ الأَيدي.

ويحملُني جناحُ حمامةٍ بيضاءَ صَوْبَ

طُفُولةٍ أُخرى. ولم أَحلُم بأني

كُنتُ أَحلُم. كُلُّ شيء واقعيٌّ. كُنتُ

أَعلَم أَنني أُلقي بنفسي جانباً ...

وأَطيرُ. سوف أكونُ ما سأَصيرُ في

الفَلَك الأَخيرِ. وكُلُّ شيء أَبيضُ،

آلبحرُ المُعَلَّقُ فوق سقف غمامةٍ

بيضاء. واللَّا شيء أَبيضُ في

سماء المُطْلَق البيضاءِ. كُنتُ، ولم

أَكُنْ. فأَنا وحيدٌ في نواحي هذه

الأَبديّة البيضاء. جئتُ قُبَيْلَ ميعادي

فلم يَظْهَرْ ملاكٌ واحدٌ ليقول لي:

«ماذا فعلتَ، هناكَ، في الدنيا؟»

ولم أَسمع هُتافَ الطيِّبينَ، ولا

أَنينَ الخاطئينَ، أَنا وحيدٌ في البياض،

أَنا وحيدٌ ...

لا شيء يُوجِعُني على باب القيامةِ.

لا الزمانُ ولا العواطفُ. لا

أُحِسُّ بخفّةِ الأشياء أَو ثِقَل

الهواجس. لم أَجد أَحداً لأَسأل:

أَين «أَينني» الآن؟ أَين مدينةُ

الموتى، وأَين أَنا؟ فلا عَدَمَ

هنا في اللا هنا ... في اللا زمان،

ولا وُجُود

وكأَنني قد مُتُّ قبل الآن ...

أَعرفُ هذه الرؤيا، وأَعرفُ أَنني

أَمضي إلى ما لَستُ أَعرفُ. رُبَّما

ما زلتُ حيّاً في مكانٍ ما، وأَعرفُ

ما أُريدُ ...

سأَصيرُ يوماً ما أُريدُ

سأَصيرُ يوماً فكرة. لا سَيْفَ يحملُها

إلى الأَرض اليباب، ولا كتابَ ...

كأَنّها مَطَرٌ على جَبلٍ تصَدَّعَ من

تَفَتُّح عُشْبةٍ،

لا القُوَّةُ انتصرتْ

ولا العَدْلُ الشريدُ

سأصير يوماً ما أُريدُ

سأصير يوماً طائراً، وأسُلُّ من عَدَمي
وجودي. كُلَّما احترَقَ الجناحانِ
اقتربتُ من الحقيقةِ، وانبعثتُ من
الرمادِ. أنا حوارُ الحالمين، عزَفْتُ
عن جَسَدي وعن نفسي لأُكمِلَ
رحلتي الأولى إلى المعنى، فأحرَقَتْني
وغاب. أنا الغيابُ. أنا السماويُّ
الطريدُ.

سأصير يوماً ما أُريدُ

سأصيرُ يوماً شاعراً،
والماءُ رَهْنُ بصيرتي. لُغتي مجازٌ
للمجاز، فلا أقولُ ولا أشيرُ
إلى مكانٍ. فالمكان خطيئتي وذريعتي.
أنا من هناك. «هُناءيَ يقفزُ
من خُطاكيَ إلى مُخَيَّلتي ...
أنا من كُنتُ أو سأكونُ
يصنعُني ويصرعُني الفضاءُ اللانهائيُّ
المديدُ.

Mural

by Mahmoud Darwish
translation by John Berger and Rena Hammami

Here is your name
said the woman
and vanished in the corridor

A hand's reach away I see heaven
a dove's white wing transporting me to another childhood
and I don't dream that I'm dreaming
Everything is real
And I meet myself at my side
And fly

I will become what will be in the final circuit
Everything is white
The sea hanging above a roof of white clouds
in the sky of the absolute white nothingness
I was and was not
Here alone at the white frontier of eternity.

I came before my hour so no angel approaches to ask:
What did you do over there in the world?
I don't hear the chorus of the righteous or wailing of sinners
I'm alone in the whiteness
alone…

At the gate of resurrection nothing hurts
neither time past nor any feeling
I don't sense the lightness of things nor the weight of appre-
hension
There's no one to ask:
where now is my where?
Where is the city of death
Where am I?
In this no-here…
no-time
and nothingness

As if I had died already
I know this story
I know that I go towards what I don't know
Perhaps I'm still alive somewhere
Aware of what I want…

One day I'll become what I want
One day I will become a thought
that no sword or book can dispatch to the wasteland
A thought equal to rain on the mountain split open by a blade
of grass
where power will not triumph
and justice is not fugitive

One day I'll become what I want
One day I'll become a bird
that plucks my being from nothingness.
As my wings burn I approach the truth
and rise from the ashes
I am the dialogue of dreamers
I shunned body and self to complete the first journey towards
meaning
but it consumed me then vanished
I am that absence
The fugitive from heaven

One day I'll become what I want
One day I'll become a poet
Water obedient to my vision
My language a metaphor for metaphors
I don't speak or indicate a place
Place is my sin and subterfuge
I am from there
My here leaps from my footsteps to my imagination…
I am from what was or will be
I was created and destroyed in the expanse of the endless void

Foreword

by The Future Guardian of the Letters

I

The documents herein are of

AN   ERA

when it was difficult for the measures of a poem to contest
the authority of a poet's identity or the tribe to which she
belonged. Sadly, it was too late for the life of a poem to just
be—to breathe. And *by* "the life of a poem" one did not mean
literally "a poem" but any possibility in writing for the imagination to *be* anonymous and free. (Like the sea.) As it was in the
letters of Carla, the letter b., in her hero worship.

At one time, the sinologist Ernest Fenollosa said it like this: As
"'Is' comes from the Aryan root as, to breathe. 'Be' is from bhu,
to grow."

At another time, the poet Wallace Stevens said it like this:

> It was how he was free. It was how his freedom came.
> It was being without description....
> ("The Latest Freedman")

And at yet another time, the poet Amiri Baraka said it like this: "What your spirit is *is* what you are, what you breathe upon your fellows. Your internal and elemental volition."

As it is, I say it among the guardians and noble scribes who have 21st century ancestors who claimed *to be*, how do I dare say it, the poet gangland(ers) of their time, whose theories and selves were quite interesting and opened new avenues down which intelligence might travel. However, as some critics of the time said, they were so obsessed with personalities and tail-sniffing and who's on first that they seemed laughable as well, if you dug deep into it. And I did—dig deep—as well. And because I did dig deep I am riddled by and heir to this conundrum now in the air around me: how do I tell their story so that it is relevant to those who don't have a dog in this fight, who know nothing of the names and tribes written herein, yet who would love to know how the imagination can be anonymous and free in a writing shaped outside of any one identity? Or, to put it very other-ly and by virtue of some questions:

> *Who was she, this figure of Carla, the letter b.? Who peopled her and why? Why did she need guarding?*
> *Why was the letter b the only evidence of her surname, and why did it come after a first name beginning with the letter c?*
> *What did her letters reveal about the figure behind her whose spirit could only be known through his creation, his breath, his great sigh, his fundamental sadness? Was this spirit complicit in a crime?*

II

As sole guardian, as only the guardian, no way did I think all these questions could be answered by the letters nor did I think these could be the only questions. But I did think this: What if at least a few of the responses invited a curiosity about whether the would-be encounters in these letters could, well, come to be? What if they could transcend the necessity of the very identities of real names in the communities of the poetry of the 20th and 21st centuries—for example, the poets named Charles

Olson and Heriberto Yépez among others—characters you might not care for or know because they were among the elite in that long since world, the best of show, as such, and as some critics said, so far up their own tail-sniffing asses?

Which is fine, if you did not care, if you did not know the poets herein, if you had no dog in their fight, if you thought: "some such gassed nonsense is this b.s." In fact, I might even agree with you if, that is, I were not implicated.

As guardian, however, *their letters* came to *me* in a case through a pneumatic tube of a wormhole and I have had no such luxury to think "some such nonsense is this" and have had no choice but to watch over their poetic kind: those whom you could find news of in the virtual world of the 21st century but who, in the words of a 19th century scribe, *I would prefer not to* publicize at this time, eons later, when the virtual worlds and their discussion boards had shut down and the letters pressed once again upon us.

For example, to whom could I tell of the kind of epistolary news which came from one Carlos b. Carlos Suarès? Some say he was a boy runaway. Or the one that got away. Whichever, as one could tell by the sound of his name, he was linked to Carla, the letter b. and had a story. Some said he was the figure who hid behind Carla's skirts and could never be himself (thus his fundamental sadness), and so could only be understood, like a poem, beyond his time, as he was a nobody in his?

(and as I am a nobody in mine)

But what did it mean to be "a nobody in his" ("as I am a nobody in mine")? *More on this question later.*

III

For now, to understand Suarès, since I am among the guardians and noble scribes who has access to this cache of letters, we must go to the question on the mind of a so-called gringo author of the time, who tried to breathe brief life into the nostrils of the Suarès no one saw. In this author's letters, we find the following *apologia*:

I desperately wanted to beget understanding in another but knew
that to reach out as myself in order to be revealed in another would
be a stretch beyond comprehension. Who, I thought, believes the au-
thor, anyway? Which is why I reached out in disguise. Was guarded.
Remained unknown. Unborn. Which is why I obsess on the love
of satire as form. Which is why I dressed up. Which is no excuse, I
know, I messed up. I should be scorned. I wanted to inspirit Carlos b.
Carlos Suarès, to be a fake Mexican scholar, whom I tried to breathe
life into but had no right. To his clothes, to his scarf, to his collar,
to his lungs-being. I'm sorry. It was not righteous. But I am not a
church. I have no collar. May I tell you why? I did it. I only obsess on
the love of satire as form. Which is no excuse. I know. It chokes me to
this day. Thank you. No more of me.

Yours,
the forsworn author

More from "the forsworn author" later. For now, it is clear he

sounded rapt and forlorn. It could be heard in the rapid and

cutthroat syntax and locution. One would have expected the

slow, pensive drawl of painstakingly wanted forgiveness for

his mistaken creation, Carlos b. Carlos *Suarès*, who was, it was

said, "a nobody in his time." But what did this mean: to be "a

nobody in his time?"

For some, it was a good sign. It meant that long ago the

rhythms of poetry *could* contest the authority of the *some-bo-*

dyness of a poet. (Imagine a society in which this one somebody breeds many—the one makes the many—who then populate a desert tribe—and then, as in the ancient of days, as in some Arabic verse traditions, the mark of a poet is how well the measured sounds of his poetry contest the authority of the tribe rather than *bow* to it.) In her time, for sure, Emily Dickinson was *an always contesting reminder of poetic anonymity in my ancestors' age of tribal trolling:* she who, in her era, bowed to no one and sent her poems in and as letters, archived as such. She who said I will see you anon but who said it like this:

> I'm Nobody! Who are you?
> Are you – Nobody – too?
> Then there's a pair of us!
> Don't tell! they'd advertise – you know!
>
> How dreary – to be – Somebody!
> How public – like a Frog –
> To tell one's name – the livelong June –
> To an admiring Bog!

This is not the time for an exegesis of her poem, and certainly not from me. But for "The Critic" it is different, at least from what I can glean from his letters *(more of how he came to be, lat-er)*. For now, we can turn to the authority with which he speaks and the arguments which he makes, and from which I crib, for Dickinson's poem:

> If a poet means to dwell in the possibility of this 19th century Dickinson poem, if a poet means to produce the measure of like to like, then *is it* hard to imagine—in the twenty-first century—a variant word choice where the poem in its time is a critique of our self-admiring own?

> How dreary – to be – Somebody!
>
> How public – like a Frog –
>
> To tell one's name – the livelong June –
>
> To an admiring *Blog*!

Is it hard to go from "bog" to "blog?" So "The Critic" goes on:

> Because ours is a time when the admiring blogs rule, and the poets can only be images of themselves, their biographies pre-cede or condition the words of their poems: the prison writings of X, the poems of queer lit extraordinaire Y, the veritable verse of Filipino-Puerto Rican poet-laureate Z, the Ju-seum poems of poets for whom Is-rael Is-real or not, the poems of any poet of any color or no-color which becomes a paradigm for pos-terity and the National Vanity—Pride needed, not to be heard right, but to be proved right.

> The vanity, even of social purpose: to see what the poem does mirrored back to us in the service of…
> so that if poetry stands in for a moral party, for a civic identity,

for the goose step that laid the golden dawn party, well, then, it is in the service of....

IV

Carla, the letter b., could be of no help to "The Critic" here,

being not comfortable in her own skin to be "in service of" to

anybody. Her letters to North American readers are no occa-

sion for an argument on behalf of anyone. She tells us some-

thing different and only wanted, like Carlos b. Carlos *Suarès*

before her, to save her hero, Heriberto Yépez (*more about the*

hero, later), from himself. Like Carlos (who was also known as

Carlo) before her, Carla, the letter b. was not meant to be, real,

nor even to be an identity or, even further, a savior, though she

could act the part, even speaking Spanish. And, of course, now

with a feminine persona, all the pestering questions started,

first and foremost: how did she come to be from Carlo, who

was also known as Carlos? To come to be was frustrating and

took on its own life, if, that is, it could be called a life, or if,

even more sadly, there was the possibility that one day some-

one would take it. James Baldwin (who sounded here like an

existential James Bond) said it like this:

> Identity would seem to be the garment with which one covers the nakedness of the self: in which case, it is best that the garment be loose, a little like the robes of the desert, through which one's nakedness can always be felt, and, sometimes, discerned. This trust in one's nakedness is all that gives one the power to change one's robes.

So it was for Carla, the letter b., who "trusted in her nakedness" and wore the changing robes of the desert against the robes of her tribe, any tribe, the tribe of poets, the tribe of gangland (ers), the tribe of family, of race and nationhood, forsaking her need to belong since she was only meant to reproduce the measure of her likeness in others. In the words of Wallace Stevens, who in his time said it like this, she warned us of the limits of identity:

> Both in nature and metaphor, identity is the vanishing point of resemblance.

And "The Critic" said it to Mr. Stevens like this:

> if the identity of a poet is the measure of his authority, and if identity becomes the vanishing point of resemblance, does it not logically follow that, if the defense of one's *identity* is the sorrowful *key* to the fate of a poem, as if it were the idea of

order at *key* west, then the measure of what a poem can be has been stilled, as metaphor, as resemblance, as correspondence as, in effect, heteronymous, as would-be, as a way out of who one was (and was to be).

V

Yes, "as would-be, as a way out of who one was," could this aphoristic movement people the mystery of Carla, the letter b., and be one reason she came to be, since behind her, so the others' letters agree, were the epistolary echoes of the Wallace Stevens poem "The Comedian as the Letter C." (And it is here we draw the curtains to reveal who Stevens, as poetic agent, may have had in mind, or in his case, insured, as the letter C, as at least one possibility: *The Critic.* And, as the letters of one Bloom off the Rose told them at the time, "we ought not to forget, he is a dead man."

Not a wanted man, but a dead man, said the Bloom off the Rose. Perhaps, being an unwanted dead man, this is why Stevens' letters to his Italian translator refer to Crispin as a plain, dull man, even as his name is cutting edge: Crispin, it goes well with, Critic. "The Critic" as tic, who can't let go of the poem. For sure, he could be a poser, a chameleon, a dead man who could rise and claim to be anybody just digging himself into someone else's skin, like a Comedian with his Barbs and Arrows, except not very funny because very academic and, well, a dead man rising and unwanted–like the poster boy for, well, a critic. In other words, unlike so many in the 20th and 21st centuries, who at the time needed to defend their pride in who they were in essence and at heart (which was odd, ironic, since, at the time, even as the people with their technologies were (like smiling goats) on the precipice of human cloning and their computer worlds on the ground floor of being inhabited by fugitive avatars, they still performed defenses of the principles of a core identity), this man had nothing of value to guard, at core. It was all just plush-for-the-Shakespearean-stage for him, this word whoring Crispin in "The Comedian as the Letter C.," whom Stevens once said could equally be "The Comedian as the Sounds of the Letter C":

> He, therefore, wrote his prolegomena,
> And, being full of the caprice, inscribed

Commingled souvenirs and prophecies.
He made a singular collation. Thus:
The natives of the rain are rainy men.

(From "The Comedian as the Letter C")

VI

Thus, as guardian, I found more intrigue in the letters of "The

Critic," who spoke of Stevens' poem like this:

In the poem, a plain man named Crispin needs a landscape to
troll, to command. Stevens seems to be Commanding him, I
would dare say logically Copulating with him, his marionette—
though it is difficult to discern author from character—in his
poems, if that wooden sexual metaphor were understood, well,
grammatically. He makes unorthodox connections, threesomes,
and with hardened authority. So he says Crispin "made a singular collation: The natives of the rain are rainy men." The natives.
The rain. Rainy men.
What should be understood is that "the poet as comedian is
both Stevens and Crispin, both an essential figure creating and
celebrating relations, and an absurd figure whose relations are
false. The poem contains 'pages of illustrations' that 'These/Two
things are one.'"(Fred Miller Robinson). Thus, "the natives of
the rain are rainy men."
This is the logic of copulation: how could it be otherwise. The
predicate is absorbed in the subject, the identity of two is fixed
as one to make another, how could "the natives of the rain" be
anything other than "rainy men."

On the other hand, what are these absurd figures and evanescent things he makes into and calls "rainy men": it seems "rainy
men" would be free of attachment, of subject and predicate,
more like the Freedman in that other Stevens poem, who says
　　　　　　　　　"I suppose there is
A doctrine to this landscape. Yet, having just

25

Escaped from the truth, the morning is color and mist,

Which is enough."

And I suppose it is enough for the rainy men as well to have
escaped from the sky, be mist fleshed, feet plodding on ground-
lessness, in tropic air or airlessness, in the end being free men
without description, heavy enough to fall under gravity yet light
enough to be like the "the forms of love" in a rainforest under
the moonlight which George Oppen openly wonders about and
cannot name when he looks out with his wife, Mary, the two
of them groping "[their] way together/Downhill in the bright/
Incredible light" wondering "whether it could be lake or fog
[they] saw" and then going together "to where it could have
wet [their] feet had it been water" And the question is: what
is this "it" in "had it been water"—what is this which will, well,
disappear here, "being full of the caprice" when "the morning is
color and mist."

VII

Thus Carla, the letter b., and whoever touches her, is—full of it:

the mist and the caprice.

"The Critic" has it right: capricious. And it seems I have

become wistful enough to see things like this, or things have

come to me like this, like these letters, as a case of not mistaken

but forsaken identities, one figure surrendering to another by chance, so here, Stevens as Crispin as "being full of the caprice"

be-coming the forms of George and Mary Oppen's love for

each other, a chance meeting of evaporators, like the gravity of

sidelong rain hitting our eyelids in the moonlight, where the

subject of one's being is the predicament of the other, and so

they go, together.

And so it is with my handling of these letters of Carla, the

letter b. and who came before or after her, that the subject of

one's being is the predicament of the other—and so they go,

together—because it is true that several times now in going

over these letters and, as one of the noble scribes referencing

them for you, I have misspelled, and so mistaken and substitut-

ed, the name Clara for Carla, the letter b., and have then erased

the error. I will no longer.

These chance errors, much like dyslexic mood chang-

es, have, I now realize, a purpose, as they reveal Carla to

be the beauty on my mind who falls into my lap as the

Hollywood anagram of the silent film star, Clara Bow

who gives me and you a pretty face and dark wavy hair to gaze

at, to bow to as a model for Carla, the letter b. At the same

time, she is someone who can never talk back, be in service of, give blowback, no matter how tempting it would be to receive it from her, to see what is on her mind. Like Karla, John le Carré's Soviet spymaster, she is one of the ghosts whose motives for being one cannot grasp, wholly, looking back as I am, as guardian. As to what Carla might want from Clara or Carlo or Carlos or others, well, none of this gives me very much to go on since even as I give you her face I have to confess, I have to come to terms with the perennial ever frustrating conundrum of the letters: their figures lead us in circles and respectfully bow in turns one to the other: Carla, the letter b., like Clara Bow—arms spread, legs akimbo, a pre-talkie—both unable to speak for themselves, both still a mystery to me.

VIII

Which brings me back to the fate of the late Carlos b. Carlos Suarès, who could never be wanted because of a huge *mix*-up, for which his author confessed his belated fundamental sorrow, in so many ways, and for which Carlos was virtually a dead man before he was born, subject to blowback.

How, you ask, can one apologize, as the author most certainly desired, for a dead man yet to be born? It is not for me to say, except to cite, once again, the divine breath of the one who desperately wants yet cannot be known through others, which I find in these letters, the author of which said it —his *apologia*—like this:

> I swore I would never confess—that the names which came to me would stay guarded. In witness protection. They were the gangland(ers) of Il Gruppo. Goodfellows. All Poets. In defense of. Another poet (his name was Charles). All on the defensive. All Irked. By one man (his name was Heriberto). A Jerk. Witless. At first. So I thought. I was wrong. No more of me. Only my shame in knowing that he was not that jerk or witless. What I thought. I'm sorry. He was not that…. I say: no more of me. I now confess: his name was Heriberto, a Mexican poet, a scholar, who irked me, us, who called ourselves Il Gruppo. It sounded strange and tough, poets as gangland boxers. But Poets often do odd things. Like call themselves "Il Gruppo" and threaten to publish an attack, as we did, on a man like this man, Heriberto, who wrote a book on a famous North American very Whit(e) Man like poet and scholar, Charles, whom he ridiculed for his mid twentieth century imperialism and his "poetics of Anglo Empire," so he framed him like a daguerreotype and thus vaulted to fame, although Il Gruppo never thought Charles was all that shallow, A Whit(e) Man poet and scholar (That argument will follow), and that Heriberto was just wrong about the Whit(e) man and his follow(ers).
> Heriberto and his allies, Il Gruppo and their allies, fought, there was a struggle, and the arguments collapsed. But the Suarès I dreamt up, well, he lay fallow and then came to, out of the scrum, to look funny and serious at the same time, like *he* was going to defend Heriberto but it was really *me* with **Il Gruppo** attacking *him* under the name of the mythical Carlos b. Carlos Suarès, clever I thought for me to be under the influence of this name which could be funny and serious at the same time

because I thought let's leave polemics behind now how boring
that would be and let there be born a golem out of the gassed
b.s. a species of dust clouded theatre of drunken vagrants a
Midsummer Night's Dream of the present poetic *polis* (police),
and let this posed Carlos come as one of them posting letters
to North American readers and be disguised as a south of the
border scholar disciple of Heriberto whom he was not, because
the whole affair turned on me, I was a maker of disciples, and
it came to light, I was, like the darkness, like the accuser, that
which I am, or others suppose that I am, the so-called gringo
mime, a maker of false disciples, which hurts me, that I could be
like that, so dark a Goodfellow who (though '*I go, I go, look how
I go, Swifter than the arrow from a Tartar's bow*') almost wound
up piercing and saddening Heriberto's and a whole people's
heart, although the miming was solely meant as thorough
loving satire, which was the form I loved, all dressed up in fine,
light satire, and I thought so too would Heriberto, like it, the
attire, at heart. This is what I thought and this is what I wrote
to Guillermo.
Why did I assume he, Heriberto, would love it? Why would he
be as smart? Why would he love the satire? Well, his writing
had worn the same attire, like a sports star lettered in the genres
of the fictive and parodic translation-criticisms (**crítica ficción**).
Made up authors. Made up critics. And so on....As I had made
up Carlos. We were brothers in make-up. **In** *crítica ficción*. So I
thought.
Well, it turns out... I was told "don't do it—don't dress up as
Carlos, it's messed up. That's no way for brothers to be. Satire
punches up, not down. You're a gringo punching down and the
people who need to can't get up. Don't you get it? They are the
others, not your brothers, they can't get up and you're punching
them down. The satire you love is the one with clothes your
kind has always worn and owned, you will reap what you have
sown. This is a crime." This is what Guillermo, a friend of Heriberto, wrote, sort of. No more of me.
I said: "This saddens me, it's my loss, Guillermo, you're right, I
own it, this is not fine, it's sordid, but it's too late to disown him,
my Carlos b. Carlos Suarès, is, already written!"
But then a voice thundered, "mark your words—he is *only* written, he is not *yet printed*, he is conceived but not yet born, so all

is not lost and it is not too late for Carlos not to come to light. Let there be no light, anon!"
And so I was saved—thank goodness by—

[Here the letter breaks off and, like a series of commas interrupting the *apologia*, there are words starting with and often emboldened by the capital letter **C** sound everywhere, most small and getting smaller and hard to decrypt. But in a parenthetical footnote, the author of the Suarès letters gives thanks to the editor of The **Shadowy** Review of **C**hicago for understanding how this chicanery will work—the gringo author disappearing into the background, all in good fun. And, then, of course, thanks for saving him. More of this later.

A side note: The word "**Shadowy**" in its title, the footnote explained, was used as homage to a magazine which, in the 1940's, in its infancy and ironically, no publisher sent in books for "review" and so, occasionally, in good fun and out of necessity, a "shady" editor reviewed a book of an Australian novelist whom he invented on the spot, in dark, blurred newsprint, of course, and in a city where the buildings cast their silhouettes on the glassy iced lakefront. That first editor said it like this:

> Perhaps the most prominent works we published were pieces by Louis-Ferdinand Celine; I believe we were his first American publisher. These came to us thanks to arrangements made by Milton Hindus who had a deep interest in discussing Celine's work and sanely recognized that before one could comment on a text the text had to exist. *I'm not so sure that's still true.*

As guardian, I noticed that even that first editor's final sounding italics recognized the future possibility of the non-existent Suarès of the Suarès letters, letters who the present editor asks permission to publish so that Carlos could, figuratively, be born among us.

> Would it be alright with you if Carlos were born among us, so to speak, if we published the two Suarès letters in two successive issues—the first letter at the end of November, or the very beginning of December, and the second letter in winter? I think if we prime our audience by "leaking" some of the second letter, and then build anticipation with the strategic serial publication of the two letters, we might create the effect among the public that we want…. I just hope we're able to give you a venue you can be happy with.
>
> (The Editor)

The author is ecstatic. "Of course, publish, let Carlos be

born! How lovely!" The footnote tells an unknown (soon to be forsworn) author, writing through a heteronym (Carlos), what that author never hears but is expressed so well here: of "creating an effect on the public," of an audience who will be "primed," of giving him a venue he "can be happy with." But then, weeks later, after agreeing to print the so-called gringo author, the editor has a change of heart:

> I'm…sorry to report that after sharing the Carlos b. Carlos Suarès material with more staffers and receiving their careful responses, and in light of the mood of the reactions I received from the bloggers I reached out to, I'm far less certain that the magazine can commit to publishing the Suarès letters.
>
> (The Editor)

The author asks himself: what's wrong? What has he done? He is a bit bewildered, feels crossed, a bit. Perhaps he looks askance, cross-eyed. I can't be sure. I imagine the letters blur in front of his eyes, which tear, and for small-minded "Staff(ers)," he reads "Staph(ers)," so that in a brief, understandably bitter moment of rejection, he dreams up grape-like clusters of people he wants to squeeze the juice out of in the light of day before asking: "why now does The **Shadowy** Review of Chicago stop Cooperating with this playful Chicanery which I, the Self-Confessed Gringo Author, Called the letters of Carlos b. Carlos Suarès?" But it is only a brief, embittered moment, to which, the gringo author learns, he has no right.

The editor makes his case, the reasonableness and revelations of which subdues the author. He explains that yes, previous emails expressed an interest in publishing the letters, but there was no agreement to run the content. Staffers scouted potential bloggers to publicize the Suarès letters and, in doing so, they discovered the troubling echo that a gringo masking as a Mexican talking of "disappearance" had, this time in the 21st century, with an ongoing humanitarian crisis south of the United States border: most recently, the vanishing of several college students.

> Mexicans were disappearing never to return, for reasons other than literary disputes. In this context, Suarès' mimicry of a borderlander takes on a sinister cast. And the malicious overtones of the attack on Heriberto Yépez throughout the letters become much more pronounced when the troubling resonance of this language is fully understood.
>
> (The Editor)

His conclusion: the Suarès letters did not engage in the kind of provocative discussion that "is transparent" enough for The **Shadowy** Review of Chicago, where, he wrote, "controversy is appreciated but only so long as it's put in the service of fair and substantive debate."

Looking back, which I suppose is my role as the future guardian, the editor was right: no way could Carlos be born into this climate. The author had gone too far, no doubt, and he knew it in his heart. He had no ground to stand on to defend this literary mimicry of a borderlander when real people were, in fact, disappearing, slipping into the real shadows. And his only thought was, to hide out of self-humiliation, to be gone, to say —I'm sorry: no more of me.

More-so, throughout this whole affair, the editor sounded noble, as he only wanted to be in the service of people who "appreciate controversy…so long as it's put in the service of fair and substantive debate." This is not to say there were not critics from the letters of the time who wondered otherwise, who somehow had access to the not yet published Suarès letters and noticed first that, when they combed the script in fine detail, there was never any direct mention of Heriberto's disappearance—in fact, in the irony of ironies, just the opposite was the case: Heriberto's shadowy *gringo enemies* were the only ones referenced as "disappeared," and I say "referenced" because the word itself was never literally (*sic*) used, only imagined and repeated by the editors of The **Shadowy** Review of Chicago, who may have cited it without correction because the whole situation incited fear in people, which was understandable, given the political context. Second, the critics judged that "to read in the service of any ideology is not…to read at all." One could see this comment, for example, in the letters of the aforementioned Bloom Off the Rose, a tired, sad, humane old creature with a bulbous nose, who would ask, as I would, briefly: how is it that, in the 21st century, the form of satire needed to be in service of anything, let alone fair, transparent debate? Was it truly the role of satire to be transparent let alone fair or correct? And he thought—this is strange. This is a strange, mysterious fate for a form.

And so it was written in the letters of the Bloom Off the Rose, is it not the fate of an author, particularly writing in this form under a heteronym, "to disappear?" And so the difficult question came to me, as scribe, as I imagine it no doubt came to the forsworn author: would writing or even merely suggesting a word other than "disappear," maybe in another language, have made a difference in this whole affair, in whether Carlos b. Carlos Suarès would be born, in whether his author was slammed and dismissed as sinister? Is this conundrum not what the forsworn author must have had in mind by having his Carlos collude with the literary form Heriberto loved—since Heriberto was always appearing under other assumed names— that all their names would vanish in time and the offensive content which followed would only be a natural extension of that form of satire they both loved and would then be gone as well, when the morning is color and mist? No harm. No foul. No punching up, no punching down. Yet this is not how it went down, since, as the author tells it, he knew he was wrong, and that he was embroiled in a huge *mix-up* of his own doing and had no choice but to get in front of the situation and hide and bury his almost creation and be saved from his own follies by the clarity of the editor of The **Shadowy** Review of Chicago

who justifiably wanted no more of the mimicry of a border-

lander, the author of which said it like this:

> no more of me thank goodness I was saved from the fake Mex-
> ican poet and scholar and mock savior I mimed, the late Carlos
> b. Carlos Suarès, me, who only tried to foolishly help Heriberto,
> hide him, save him from his enemies which was no excuse I
> know for the act of miming him, who had to move on up or
> down on his own, trans-genderfly, Carlos who had to become
> Carla, the letter b. To be free. Like Shakespeare, who the Bloom
> off the Rose said wrote "bisexually because he wrote universal-
> ly." I'm sorry. No more of me. Anon.
> Yours,
> the forsworn author

IX

How could that be, though? To soon be free, yes, but to be

even more anonymous than he already was, now moonwalk-

ing even further into the shadows to find refuge in Carla, the

letter b., she who had to be taken from him like a pure Holly-

wood-sexed rib and so re-named so as to be so guarded so that

he, Carlos b. Carlos Suarès and the forsworn author behind

Carlos b. Carlos Suarès, would be rescued and sworn to secrecy

and never be seen? How complicated this would be if it were

a yellowy chalked crime scene, bones under bones of names,

39

as if these names had no choice but to be perpetually erased, in hiding, since Satire as the Loving Form Of Cross Talking Identities Would Never Do Well in the Era Which Was in Service of I Need to Be That Who I Say I Am at the Center of the Universe A Man Would Never Do Well to Appear Like a Joker [in that era any time of year] at the risk of blowback, that word which their Wiki Wiki sources at the time warned them was "originally Central Intelligence Agency (master/mistress spymaster organization) currency, internal coinage denoting the unintended, harmful consequences—to friendly populations." In this case, blowback from the people of North America towards their neighbors in The Mexican Republic of Letters.

So why, the author thought, be a borderline funny gringo man who makes up disciples south of the border? Why risk blowback against the people of The Mexican Republic whom he loved and the Heriberto whom he paid homage to if all that was wanted was friendly transparency on a beautiful, clear sunny day. So he decided to make it right, to confess his name to everyone—"*I am that I am the guilty forsworn author man*"—for the sake of friendly transparency on a beautiful, sunny afternoon by the sea, which was born of the meaning of another (this time Japanese-Persian poet's) name, Harumi, on a humid day in July. And he concluded: Why, as Laura, the letter R. once wrote in another era, and as the author knew too well, have this literary border patrol, "this wall, this poet-like address," between the author and Heriberto since, in the end, the fundamental sadness and real blowback would only be, alas, that they would never meet?

X

Even, however, if they had indeed met, even if they could have been allies in dialogue or dogs in the same fight over the long history and tradition of heteronymic poetics which could part like rain clouds heretofore unopened portals of time and space, the fact was that none of them as names would really matter in the future, only the conundrum in which they each played a role. That conundrum can now be seen reflected in a photograph of one of the screenshots of the time, a poem the author confessed to memorizing, in which an anonymous Sufi poet asks what happens

> when one breathes life into a character you want to see
> all one's will in, a character who can never in
> the end, be
>
> of his elemental volition
>
> Near
>
> My will, *ta'wil*,
> to produce a measure of like until
> I disappear

And the forsworn author, upon seeing the poem, followed its

logic and so wrote:

> So I did. Disappear. Took a breath in. Took a breath out. James
> Baldwin said it like this: "The poetic trick, so to speak, is to be
> within the experience and outside it at the same time." Which
> is why I love the satire as form. But it failed. I was inside only
> the form of it. So, too, Heriberto. Our fundamental sadness. To
> never meet except in the ideal form of it. I'm sorry. No more of
> me. Only Carla, the letter b.

XI

Who has been guarded all along and who, as I look back from this distance at the early 21ˢᵗ century republic of North American letters and its scribes, I have only seen in textual skin prints *sans* that era's virtual lenses. In the ultimate of paradoxes, this, our world, has been cut off from the wirelesses of their time, when the admiring blogs burnt out, except for a few illuminations, "screen shots" as they were framed then, re-shot and exposed to light as grainy salt print photographs once the systems went down and the discussion boards closed and everyone pressed on us the guardianship of the letters.

If the messages on the shot prints revealed anything, perhaps it was something about the how a poet's words could bow to and give meaning to the language of the tribe at the same time as echoing a transcendent counter-voice beyond it, the trick being to be within the experience of the tribal name and still be outside it. Curiously, this double role could be seen in the letters of the 20ᵗʰ century Algerian poet, Jean Sénac, who had movingly transformed the French poet Mallarmé's idea of the individual poet giving "meaning" to the words of the "primitive" tribe—the poet, thus, as forward looking future guardian of the words—into the poet's voice absorbing the meanings of the rallying cries and chants and songs of the Algerian tribes caught up in the midst of a revolution. The poet as ultimate outsider—where "as long as the individual is hindered in his claim of total freedom, poetry will guard the outposts and brandish the torches"—and as true to the "self" of the tribe: the poet surrendering himself to something beyond himself.

One could see some of this played out, for example, in letters the forsworn author wrote to The Tribe of John, also known as The New York School of Poets. In one letter, he hoped against hope for a word of praise for *The Letters of Carla, the letter b.* once they were published, but knowing this would be impossible and more likely would be just another way of saying farewell:

Dear John,
This is the third and last time I am writing, where I ask for your word and then I let go. Of you.
I was encouraged by David S. to send you excerpts from my

new book, which includes *The Letters of Carla, the letter b.* and which David told me to tell you has his full support. I am asking you to write a blurb. I think you will take to the MS. It has the quality of a Jacques Tati picture, the kind one finds in your poetry. But first a brief story.

In the summer of 1978, my wife and I lived on 333 West 19th Street, between 8th and 9thAvenues. It was lined with one tree. At the time, I was a young (26 year old) poet, more than a bit introverted, who found out that you lived a few blocks away and walked to your apartment with a manuscript in hand, saw the doorman at your towering London Towne House, thought of Kafka's "Before the Law," and asked: "would it be possible for you to give this to Mr. Ashbery?" mThe doorman quickly said, "soon, but not at this moment, Mr. Ashbery is not presently in," and I turned around and sheepishly headed back to my 5th floor walk-up.

34 years later I tried again, with another MS—this time by post from San Francisco—hoping Kafka's parable was a distant memory. It wasn't. Again, I never heard from you.

If today, the third time, cannot be the charm, I say: no more of me. I say: "well, here's another fine mess you've gotten me into." I say: this is why I became forsworn. Anon.

Yours,

the forsworn author

Needless to say, the third time was no charm, and even the walk-up had been demolished, so the letter said. Further, in another part of the letter, the author wondered what exactly was the relation between the members of this tribe and how accurately they were billed? Did they take loyalty oaths, he asked, which was strange, of course, to ask poets to take loyalty oaths, loyalty to what or whom, and would these include blood spilling on cards bearing the likenesses of saints and then set afire?

He reasoned thus: Yes, they were true to their name, The New York School, being urban and serious yet ironic just like the people of New York, but their very lives were foreign to the very same name, The New York School. Should not their history matter even somewhat in relation to the school they were called to be a part of or could a poet (or more likely a critic) just make up any name to sound important without being held accountable by events in one's real life—thus, the author's plaint: the demand for oaths, for fidelity to the name. It was clear no poets in this self-important "school" were asked to bare their New York, New York identity cards when reading

their verse—they were in fact outsiders, nomads in the city—
nor when reading their verse did they recite the numbers of
the public school (P.S.) from which they graduated. (Of course,
this is exactly what the forsworn author felt compelled to
confess at public readings, articulate, as proof of long standing residence, the letters and numbers of the schools he had
attended as a boy—P.S. 117, P.S. 217 in Queens—where those
who were called the NY School had never been.) The author's
conundrum was well-known: on the one hand, he desired to be
integrated into this school since he really *was* "a graduate" from
New York and so dreamt of composing according to that city's
poetic tradition, but on the other hand he did no less than contest the authority of this tribe every time he admitted to how
un-serious and un-important and lacking in irony he really was
to be considered a member in good standing of this school.
What could he do and what did it all mean for the author and
his tribe of nomads, if he even had one, that is?

XII

So he asked a question: what did it mean to compose according to a tradition, as in some Arabic verse? What did it mean for future poets and guardians? The answer was in the Arabic word for poetry, *shi'r*, "song," in which beauty and knowledge dwelled. The poet, therefore, sang past and present knowledge which someone in the future discovered for *his* tribe, someone who in remembrance could write back towards what was "originally" recorded and then forward a likeness of that knowledge even further into the future. This was how knowledge multiplied and how the word *shi'r* echoed as both song as it is and song as heard in the simple expression, *layta sh'iri*, meaning "I wish to know" and, further, "I wish you could know." One waited for the poem in the desire to know. One waited for centuries to discover that the transformations of knowledge which came through the poem worked like the Arabic word for "meter" (*bahr*), meaning "sea," the recurrence of measured sounds, the likeness of waves turning one on the other as one then went down to the ship and waited on the shore in the desire to know, to be insured by and be inspired by and be known by a poem from the past or the future which began "She sang beyond the genius of the sea," wondering: what could that mean if the genius of the sea was the measure of poetry itself? What could it mean for a poet to sing beyond it, beyond even the name of its calling, its genius, where genius is spirit which guards the house, or is one of two spirits, benevolent and malevolent, author and heteronym, attending a person across his life, beyond even the name of his calling?

XIII

The answer seemed no less than a bridge between the Continental and Arabic traditions of poetry, and it raised the question: what was being said about the relation between the author and *his* tribe in the cache of letters in front of me, which included one screen shot of bards in moist beards and dressed in humid rags of smoking jackets. They appeared holding rubber clubs standing in profile against high white walls and who looked like they liked to rule like gangs do, through "the word." As in "the word was out." Or: "just say the word." As if they were after—someone.

The letters tell us: They would hang with each other. They would be hung up on each other, like quarreling lovers. They sang supreme fictions. In a word, they could be—**Gang, Cartel, Cabal, Il Gruppo.** There is another screen shot with their name:

Il Gruppo

Il Gruppo, Algerians, New York School: in the letters of the time, the names didn't matter. They had each other's backs. But who were they, really? In the case of Il Gruppo, according to the author, we learned they were formed against one in a posse of poets, one Heriberto Yépez (although his name does not matter), who took on the person of the poet Charles Olson (although his name does not matter), calling him the great imperial paleface whose poetry shrieked empire (which does not matter). Some of the screen shots tell us that there was no such group: "There is no Il Gruppo," said Guillermo (although his name does not matter). "It's one gringo's privileged excuse to personally attack the Mexican Heriberto Yépez for daring to critique the North American Charles Olson." Other screen shots say the poets took measures to stop him. Still others said it was all a big joke, given the happenings of the times: think of it, a group of poets acting like gangland(ers) when the doings of escaped drug lords carried the day, when either "El Chapo" or James "Whitey" Bulgar was the word of the hour. Or think of it: At the same moment, and as we learn from the letters and screen shots of the times, the antennae of some entity called ME TV got caught up in a satellite *mix-up* and, on Pride Day, in order to appear to be the antennae of the race, had aired the lost Latino episode of *Leave it to Beaver*, sub-titled *Mex I Am that which I am*, where "Wally and 'the Beav,' like Popeye the Sailor Man, all puffed up on taco spinach blintzes, discover their Mexican-Jewish roots, bike down to Tijuana, scale the

Israeli American aligned wall to make birthright and live it to believe it...."

Yes, one has to believe, they were strange times: many names, many games, many pleasures, many prides, many wines...
And one wondered: what did the future hold for these letters to North American readers? What was the end game of the author, who came under the name of Carla the letter b., among others. Certainly, it was not through polemical argument to exclusively defend a poet's honor—either one Charles Olson or one Heriberto Yépez, each of whose work could fend for itself over time. Nor was it to defend their tribes. Then what was it?

Perhaps it was, in fact or through fable, through acts of imagination, to have the poets and their tribes go at it, *mix it up.* To make something new and astonished and anonymous of their persons and places, their remembrances and resemblances, in the documents herein, soon coming from the voice of Carla, the letter b., the tale of whose letters I give to you, as I give myself up to her: Now. No more of me. Anon.

HERO WORSHIP: AN OPEN LETTER TO NORTH AMERICAN READERS

The View re: my Tijuana Hero, Heriberto Yépez (and his
Imperial Fantasy, Sir Charles Olson), now strangely honoring (or not) his hero, Charles Olson, at the June, 2015
Berkeley Poetry Conference, commemorating the anniversa-
ry of the July, 1965 Berkeley Poetry Conference
(or not)
Since Any Utopian Vision Should Be Without Panel
or Place
               by Carla, the letter b.

For Eddie D.

I write this letter from the *North by Northwest* and I come
from the Middle of the Middle East and there are a few from
the Global South who know me as Carla, the letter b. (once

Carlo b. Carlo to you), fabled descendant of the great Egyptian-French Kabbalist, Carlo Giuseppe Suarès, but I digress. No doubt, I contain multitudes because I am always talking. "Americans are easy pickins," I said to my friend, John, as if I could have heard it in dreamtime from my hero, Heriberto (Hache, the letter "H"), in Spanglish ("Spanglish, our double happiness, our double struggle" writes Heriberto Yépez), when John and I were driving one day, after he had picked me up at the palatial home I worked at for a few dollars for the one known as "the kind scholar of SoCal," who had in her generosity whisked me away on a free ride, so to speak—*as I was always speaking in a language and through a name not my own*—by running me to the orange groves of SoCal to be, yes, a scholar, a graduate studies student (on scholarship) in American Literature (my thanks to her for the money for my intellectual training), soon to be schooled up North in what the poet Robert Duncan called in 1965 *The Multiversity* of Berkeley, California:

Not men but heads of the hydra

　　his false faces in which

        authority lies

   hired minds of private interests

        over us

        Here: Kerr (behind him, heads of the Bank of America

   the Tribune,

   heads of usury, heads of war)

        the worm's   mouthpiece   spreads

   what it wishes   its own

        false news:

I admired this Duncan for calling out the university adminis-

tration and faculty of 1965 and I was pleased because I thought

how far from these exclusively "hired minds" of men were we

today, in 2015, since we could be men and not men, at what

I had heard would be the new Berkeley Poetry Conference,

which would commemorate the 1965 Berkeley Poetry Confer-

ence. I had heard that in its homage it would be different from

back then: this generation of faculty and students would finally

"address the gender and racial biases of the original confer-

ence, to identify poets who would help lead diverse, challeng-
ing conversations and present work that embodied a range of
geographical, aesthetic, and social concerns." I was pleased by
the program. Yet I wondered: I remembered the poet, Carlos
Williams. I remembered he said "it is difficult/to get the news
from poems,/but men die miserably every day/for lack/of
what is found there," and I did not want to be lackluster and I
did not want to be lacking and I wanted to find the real news
of *The Times* behind the program and to be true to my near
North American namesake, Carlos.

Yet, as I said, I was pleased. I knew that, unlike those poets in
1965, there seemed to be a pointedness of diversity in who was
chosen this time, obedient to what scholars in the *North and
South* have come to raise as the question of *la raza*, the race
question, or the feminine man question, which was close to me.
Carla, the letter b., once Carlo b. Carlo, who could be like *Carlo
Giuseppe Suarès,* who believed we could go either way and could
have come from the trans-lettered Q'abala Tree, or from that
which I learned in my graduate school came from the Greeks,

the ethnos, the ethnicity question, which is like the Palestinian question, the Negro question, the Jewish question, the Indian question, and what I had heard was the poetry of witness question and the Place of Conceptual Witless Whiteness question—I discovered there are so many questions.

And I was content, although some voices warned me about my satisfiedness: one warned me in his own language that news of diversity and tolerance could, he wrote, "occlude a culture of craft professionalism suffused with a light drab of poetic secularity": that "unlike the *unaffiliated* tribe of 'poet-seers' in 1965—Duncan, Dorn, Wieners, Olson, Spicer—this current tribe of 'poet-critics, needing jobs of course, were *affiliated* with 'the academy,' as they continued to labor within the North American university creative writing provinces" (one of these warning shots from the mast came from the scholar, Mr. al-Quala, who would say: "We have pretty much come to the point of removing poetry from knowledge, and sticking it in the creative writing department"). And another voice warned me: "do you really think you will see visionaries here, at The *Multi-*

versity of Berkeley, in 2015, as some had seen seers in '65?"

Perhaps, I thought, I would. Why not? Perhaps someone would

have the true vision of *una escuela de poesia*, not of people pan-

eled up against the walls in a conference reading from pre-or-

dained academic categories, so unlike 1965, when LeRoi Jones

(Amiri Baraka) refused to appear as a black man and asked

Edward Dorn (his "The Poet, The People, The Spirit" as no

category, I was told), to go for him, which he did and recalled,

later:

> I was *not actually asked* to *attend* the *Berkeley conference* of the
> *summer* of *1965, but went* as a *substitute forced* on the *organi-*
> *zation* of the *conference* by *LeRoi Jones,* who *had begun* to *with-*
> *draw* from *such contact.* And that's how I went as an Indian.

Strangely enough, a beautiful letter in this true "school" spirit

came my way, as if from Spicer's letters to Lorca, from one

Alana Siegel, who called for a school of poetry in the com-

mons which "could meet [our desires] of imagination and

humanity." Her letter, she wrote, was inspired by no less than

"the entire incoming class of MFA students at USC [who had

just] dropped out. This act," she wrote, "inspired [her] letter, to

think from the malevolence of what has been constructed and

perpetuated, and the fiery individuals who left it!"

> *We invite everyone* to *reach out* to *us* with *proposals, invitations* and *strategies* of *their own, dreams not* of *creating* a *"better" institution, but devising new spaces* for collective weirdness and joy.

Yes, if the spirit of these fiery individuals who had "dropped out" could be captured in June, 2015, then we would no doubt hear the echoes of another time and space for poetry, as *my friend Lorenzo*, the love of "Jack(Spicer)'s" language, had reminded me happened in July of 1965 when the *North by Northeast* beach of San Francisco did cast a sort of cold eye on the compassed authority of the Multiversity of Berkeley when "Jack" appeared there, only to drop out a month later, dead in August in the poverty ward of San Francisco General Hospital, with the sweet guitar and voice lament of Trini Lopez's lovely lemon tree song still strong in his heart, "part of Jack's essential view of the world," Lorenzo told me, "the anguish of approaching the beautiful to find it essentially untouchable, although the big song for Jack on Gino's jukebox was *Quando Calienta el Sol.*" Ah, yes, "when the sun was hot," translated in the North as "love me with all your heart." It was, Lorenzo told me, what

Jack and Lorenzo and Trini and García Lorca imagined as the Real they had in common—strange, drunken bedfellows who would love each other with all their hearts and correspond "in every place and every time [where Trini's lemon could] become this lemon, or it may even become this piece of washed up seaweed, or this particular color of gray in this ocean. One did not need to imagine that lemon; one needed to discover it," but where? Under whose authority? At what "school" of the future could these things sing and correspond. Ah, yes, it could be sad and lovely with heroes in common, but I digress.

Who knows how these things wash out? I only knew that on the one day of rain in May 2015 during a decade long drought, I was forced to take cover and think: under what open umbrella of tolerance would this generation's news appear, where would the authority of their facts lie? "Well, Americans," I said, because I was always talking, "they're friendly and they don't judge and you can say anything to them, they never look back to check the facts," which is fine by me, let it be, I told John, because I was forward thinking just like them and I was remembering that fine line of the North American poet, Charles Olson (who I discovered was also at the Berkeley conference in 1965)—when I was watching a film where he had this *crazy* straight-ahead gaze in his eyes and drove off in his car which had no reverse gear, and he was asked, why do you do it, that's *crazy, man*: "Well, I like it that way: my philosophy has always been: never look backwards." Maybe that's who the austere New England poet, Robert Creeley, had in mind when he wrote:

> Drive, he sd, for
> Christ's sake, look
> Out where yr going

Anyway, I thought, Americans—North Americans to be specific—are easy pickins, these days, particularly the liberal avant-garde ones guarding the Conferences of the Academy— we call them the avant-garde(rs). I discovered there would be no need to show these avant-garde(rs) a researcher's credentials. Take what my hero has done, the poet from Tijuana, Heriberto Yépez, who would appear at the June 2015 Berkeley conference (and then—like Jones in '65—refused to appear because of the *La Raza* question), and whose book, *El imperio de la neomemoria*, translated as *The Empire of Neomemory* by a collective of translators for a publishing venture called Chain Links, had been making the rounds for a few years to make this point so well. That point, as I had kept in my memory after reading a text somewhere by *Northern* scholars, was twofold: "1) concerning his theoretical fantasy about the imperialism behind Charles Olson's work and 2) the image North Americans want to guard and keep and project when they take in a critique of their nation's politics to appease their consciences." "This work," so write the publishers and editors (Chain Links) of Heriberto's book, "is a dismantling of Olson, and of empire, and yet it is also clearly an inside job, a book that could only be written by someone who had spent hours thinking with and through—and beyond—Olson."

Yes, my Heriberto has spent hours thinking so way beyond Olson that his thinking is beyond belief, which is fine because Heriberto can be funny at times, a merry prankster, the Yépez yapping I am proud of (who else would tell me that *"'the first characteristic of the Mexican body is that it transcends colonialism; it is an unknown body' and then disappear, no longer remains, becomes unknown,"* which brings me to the second point about what my hero has accomplished: he can make you dupes of your own gringo guilt and turn authoritative, academic avant-garde(rs) upside down (as one of your black Americans, not Black Mountain College Americans, Diana Ross, sings it) and, like the bandit Gold Hat hectoring Mr. Dobbs in B. Traven's and John Huston's *The Treasure of the Sierra Madre*, in the northern desire for a south of the border perspective on how *anglo* poets are, as Fidel would say, *el colonialismo y imperialismo del norte*, you will accept Heriberto, in fact, you will be *simpatico* and take his word.

This is what Heriberto, my hero, has done to make you fall for him. He has done it with theory, theory even he knows has no foundation in reality:

> *Right now I'm studying a master's degree in psychotherapy. The first book I reread before getting into that was The Myth of Psychotheraphy by Thomas Szasz, so I won't say I believe in what I'm doing.*

But who cares? I don't believe in writing either.
I *pursue both activities anyway—without believing* in *them—because* from a *very young age* I *learned any praxis* is *better than actual reality.*

     — *The True Length of Neo-Emotionalism (A Short Story)* or

        Heriberto Yépez: *THE TRUE LENGTH OF NEO*

So why would readers believe what he says about Charles Olson? He even confesses straight up: "I am not interested in Olson." How transparent can one's motives be? "Olson in and of himself does not interest me; I am interested in his character as a microanalogy for decoding the psychopoetics of Empire." My friend, the thick moustached Chiapas poet Juan Hirsch Luria, known as "*el hombre* Tzimtzum" among the bearded mountain mystics, has written me:

> "Oh, yeah, Heriberto, I've heard of him. He's a fucking riot, his theories are crazy but interesting even though he doesn't know shit 'bout Olson *el polis hombre*, which is great, I mean he's fun to have at a party, for a few minutes, like he's doing shaman tricks: I mean he's got this new book on Carlos Olson that the North Americans are taking seriously, but even he knows it's a crock—"*eso some pretty hilarious caca there hombre*" I say—cause he's calling the big American Olson a sexual impotent—hitting him in his post-modern *polis* nuts, so to speak—an emissary of Empire, who lived and studied with the Mayans only to steal and freeze their sense of inhabiting multiple times into a conquistador's North American expansionist space, also suggesting he's an apologist for fascism (cause Olson, so Heriberto says,

64

managed to simulate that he had understood a culture by de-
*scribing...*how it "mixed" with his own. *He simulated contact*
through the *hybrid. He thus gave life* to a *new avatar* of *kitsch,*
the *happy-hybrid, possibly only* in the *mind* of the *remixer.*
But the mix of the one and the other is fascism itself. Fascism goes
hand in *hand* with *kitsch because they* are *two sides* of the *same*
false coin. (The *coin* that *pretends* to be *another.*) *Fascism is re-*
mix" –

(*The Empire of Neomemory, pgs. CXVII-CXIX*)

You can tell from the start Heriberto is lying through his teeth.
How do we know? Well, he says he is not interested in Charles
Olson, in his Carlos, but the fact is he's obsessed by him— Are
you joking me, he *fawns* and *fantasizes* over him. He wants to
breathe through and kill daddy poet at the same time. ("Daddy,
Daddy, you bastard, I'm through.") Ironically, he'll do what no
academic before him could: put the big guy on the map.
Those avant private college poet boys and girls in the poet biz
will eat it up in the States, where they're so repressed they want
so desperately to believe anyone who will fetishize (or give
him fascist eyes) and kill their father, any father, and Olson *el*

grandioso hombre is a ripe target, cause he's the breath on the big dick they can't get a hold of, if you know what I mean."

From a feminine man perspective, I know what he means. It's *satisfying* how Luria reads it: what the *Norte-Americanos* don't really know about their own poets, in this case Olson, is that someone from south of the border can get away with saying just about anything and no one will check, or, as I like to put it, give blowback. You could call this their "Olsonian inertia," so Heriberto would phrase it. Good for Heriberto: if he really knows the facts of Olson's life and is ignoring them in search of a theory to prank Americans—more power to him. Or if he doesn't know the facts, which I think is more likely (I mean— why would he even bother if he just wanted to do *a parody*), so much the better, no one will be the wiser. Either way, it doesn't matter: he makes the point, and the *North Americans* look a bit guarded defending him. I applaud Heriberto. He realizes the effects of theory, which is why he can say anything, and why he confesses he won't have any sex:

In *reality things work very differently.* And *if sex happens, some-*

times other things also happen, like kids, love. In *theory-world there* are *no consequences / just* hypothesis

(*The True Length of Neo-Emotionalism (A Short Story) or Heriberto Yépez: THE TRUE LENGTH OF NEO*)

"In theory world there are no consequences": I can imagine Heriberto telling you:

> I will stage you a theoretical monster, one Charles Olson, be-
> cause you don't know the facts, and you want to fit the big man
> into the sexist authoritarian archetype you have of him ('look at
> how he harassed women,' you will say), and in your tolerance to
> accept me as a literary representative provocateur of my people
> as victims of literary border patrols, you will accept my facts
> about the evil paleface, although I'm just making them up as I go
> along… you don't even notice that I use the word "imperialism"
> without in my book referring to any specific historical instances
> or events. I can create the bogey-man Olson to carry that word
> into his practice, I can make 'projective verse' a military manifes-
> to. I can ignore all the salient facts and relationships of Olson's
> life. I can say the Holocaust was fiction, Saddam is Hitler, 9/11
> is Pearl Harbor. I can turn water to wine, and, well, if only not to
> offend me, you Americans will say "he has a right to his perspec-
> tive; we need to learn to see ourselves from the point of view of
> '*the other*.'" A win-win for me. Even the Mexican government
> will sponsor my trips to conferences up North so that I have
> the *Norte-Americanos* in crisis and lit-quaking in their books or
> wondering how I will stage the drunken paleface of an Olson 50
> years after he staggered across the Berkeley stage.

And, if that is not enough to warn *North American* leftist anti-imperialist types of Heriberto's aesthetically rich theoretical fantasies, readers who will actually read and take seriously almost 300 pages of his riddled-with-errors, imaginary-Olson text, well, the joke, Heriberto says, is on you, refracted in a trickster text published years earlier by the same editors who may be in good faith or maybe not (who knows, their intentions no doubt were good), who printed the translation of the possibly fraudulent Olson scholarship in *El imperio de la neomemoria*. Way back in 2002, Heriberto winked at all of us—about his follies:

> In recent years, I have been involved in translation-criticism experiments involving certain types of critical fantasies in which I mix real interpretation with secret self-parody or even readers'/editors' deliberate deceptions. I have succeeded, for example, in getting non-real "criticisms" (heteronomy) or supposed translations published in major magazines, or in simply developing concepts or applying points of view in which I don't actually believe, systematically attributing false quotes to real authors or manipulating data, mixing unknown fictional authors in with canonical ones — in short, considering criticism, at every point, to be fictional prose. I write fictive and parodic translation-criticism (*crítica-ficción*) without revealing it to the readers of the books or magazines that have published those essays or pseudo-translations. In many cases my use of fiction is simply indistinguishable from my true beliefs. Even though most of the time you wouldn't know it from reading my texts, I always write criticism from an insincere point of view, as a way to destroy the confidence and authority we give to the critic as a literary subject or credible voice.
>
> *(Text, Lies, and Role-Playing*, published in *Chain* 9, 2002)

So there you have it: the *crítica-ficción* jig's (or is it the giggles are) up. You, dear North American *avant-garde(rs)*, who have taken Heriberto's Olson "bio that explains empire" seriously have just been had. Maybe, like me, you know this, or maybe you don't—what does it matter? (It's all good and all in fun.) You have been taken for a ride. You have just given him your authority. But the question remains: Why would readers believe what my literary make-up artist says about Charles Olson? Because he's got image conscious avant-garde(rs) from the North and the South by the balls and he knows it. As someone cool enough to be branded an avant-garde provocateur Mexican poet—I remember my niece once saying that what never stops through life, is that everyone wants to sit next to the cool kid in school—he can get away with claiming Charles Olson as a colonialist serving empire, only because the *anglos* in their tolerance are too afraid not to welcome "a Mexican perspective," their words justifying the attack by saying "Olson himself is not really the target but U. S. expansionism, in all its cultural forms, is…."Of course. Brilliant. My hero, Heriberto. A "know nothing" Olson scholar. And, ironically, if the more liberal gringos are told this could be a joke, the more sensitive they get and say, no, "he's serious, he's a serious scholar," the more they take Heriberto at his word, as long as he gets to kill their fathers, their families ("families are artificial structures" he says), through theory, as long as he plays his anti-imperial role as oppressed Mexicano. As my sister, the insistent "Carla, the double lettered b. b." said to me, "the more you get under the skin of the *North Americans* the more literal they get defending their agenda. Or, put another way, the more they're taken for a ride, the more they talk about the rights of the person taking them for the ride." Call it their inertia.

So *the jig's up*: because if you don't know the salient facts of Olson's life, which are just the opposite of what Heriberto claims and which Heriberto could secretly know (although I doubt it)—as Juan Hirsch Luria wrote me, "Heriberto is lying when he says he's not interested in Olson, since he's, well, obsessed by him—Are you joking me, he *fawns* and *fantasizes* over him"— then it don't amount to a hill of beans. Even Heriberto would agree—that in a time of crisis, that when poetry is in a time of crisis—strangely, this sounded similar to one of the subjects, "Poetry and the Rhetoric of Crisis," at the new Berkeley conference—then as Mexican popular culture says: "No te hagas pato" (lit. *Don't make yourself a duck*, meaning, don't pretend you are not you, don't turn into a third person in order to not assume the responsibilities of knowing you are the person you accuse, don't become 3 in order to not accept you are both 1 and 2). Which is why, in time, I would plead with Heriberto in order to protect him, plead with him to take responsibility for himself, to not be "the other": "No te hagas sitting pato, por favor" (lit. *don't make yourself the sitting duck*), I told him. "Don't hide. , Heriberto, Hache (the letter "H" in Spanish), be true to me, Carla, the letter b.," as if our motifs could be in natural correspondence, H and b, a musical cryptogram, so to speak, as if we could be singing under a lemon tree.

And if, as Heriberto writes, "Iraq… is Bush's way to hide, he is the crisis itself," then perhaps "Olson is Heriberto's way to hide that he, Heriberto, is himself the crisis." Which makes me sad. To know these facts about Heriberto, who himself admits that he "came all the way from Mexico [to Berkeley] with nothing to say."

And then—this is what is funny, I mean not ha ha, but curious funny—that the time of crisis came when Heriberto really did, not in theory but in reality, wind up with nothing to say in Berkeley since he never came and refused to appear. So he resigned—he likes to do that, resign, re-sign, arrive and leave under a different name at times because of *La Raza* question: that is, because a poet of whiteness was to be paneled with him at the place of the Berkeley conference, and because she was tweeting racist "mammy" tweets among others, this had made him resign from Berkeley under his own name, which name I knew he, Heriberto, Hache (the letter "H" in Spanish), was always giving up the letters of for one reason or another (*por hache o por be*) and trying on others until he disappeared, so it was no big deal, although it was for the *North Americans* who, like me, had loved him and published him and been chained to him and read his imperial fantasy of Charles Olson with admiration, who were really sparring with him just like the poet of whiteness, he said, as if they were standing like imperial fighters in her place, so to speak, so I heard Heriberto had said, you "gringpo morons, [I am accusing] the whole system of being co-opted and being a manipulating system to promote neo-liberal agents," he said, when before this day they were more innocent avant-garde(rs)—somewhere I had once heard James Baldwin saying "It is the innocence which constitutes the crime"—who had welcomed him with open arms (and whom he welcomed back) with sympathy as an oppressed *Mexica-no* charging up the Black Mountain impaling the great imperial paleface, Charles Olson. Well, Heriberto believed the *Norte-Americanos* singled out this woman poet of whiteness at Berkeley to save their own ass at the conference and so he turned on them and refused to appear to be always talking and so he wanted to put them in their place, so to speak, which was ironical, because the conference was meant to place this progressive conference in place of the exclusively White Paleface one in the year of 1965, since this one was announced to be Diverse, and it was, for a few weeks, announced as just that—wonderfully Diverse, pointedly—and I was pleased, but then the day came and it was not and I was not, pleased, as me, Carla, the letter b., had wanted it to be since others, well, the diverse ones and the not so diverse ones cancelled and disappeared like bees, flew out of that place with Heriberto and did not appear because they were asking why, here, in this so-called Diverse Place & Time, where they were invited, was this Conceptual Witless Whiteness Person Pointedly not Impaled but allowed to tweet among them, and I asked why, indeed, because I was in need of answers but also wondering why was not someone sent in like the clowns in Heriberto's place, the way Jones in '65 sent Edward Dorn, why was no one coming in the spirit of the people and in the spirit of a poet like Eddie D., "and that's how I went as an Indian," he said, to talk about the Real in the Poetry Commons to talk about The Poet, The People The Spirit and Color. Or how that piece of lemon could become this particular color of gray in the ocean when stones had been thrown where some poets of color and some poets of no color earnestly remained and some earnestly refused to appear as one color or another one and then before we knew it and all at once some were "gone with the wind" and the *Norte-Ameri-*

canos on the one day of rain in May 2015 during a decade long drought were forced to take cover and think: "under what open umbrella would this news appear, where would the authority of our facts lie," well nowhere, since once again they were left holding the umbrella, and it collapsed, and the Place Flooded, and frankly no one wanted to have the conference day have its say, everyone was washed up, exhausted, no one wanted to put humpty dumpty together again, and the Place Flooded almost to South of the Border, beyond Houston beyond Mr. Dobbs beyond B. Traven and then, like a miracle, while so many were rescinding the waters were receding and others rose up bobbing with umbrellas and mouthing "let's re-group" so they re-grouped because the North American agents were always re-grouping and talking of *blowback* and saying "get us witness-es, back-up singers, poets of some color for 'the other' poets of some color, and for the poets of no color (we only have 4 white poets remaining) who left us in this Place, drowning, get us witnesses whom we can impanel and cross talk and we'll call it, why not, Cross Talk, Color and Composition, to position our poets of color like new constellations in conversation," at this

cross talk conference which took the place of the conference
which had been planned it was said to "address the gender
and racial biases of the original," what else, conference in the
summer of 1965 but which obviously could not be because this
one came with racist mammy tweets and failed as it was imagined which saddened them they said and which it now turned
out to be the pointed purpose of the cross talk to amend ("the
conference to end all conferences" they said) which would not
be a referendum on race even as some poets had been impaled
and had raced out of the place like Heriberto himself who I
heard had said:

> I was invited to the Berkeley Poetry Conference and I *accepted*
> *the invitation* (*not without some personal hesitancy: am I a poet*
> *in the (North-) "American" How to participate in an event with*
> *a genealogical spirit and not contribute to its Olsonian inertia?*)
> And amidst these ongoing questions, *the Vanessa Place scandal*
> *happened and I decided I had to cancel—not because she was going*
> *to be there*

to save their ass because they were always cross talking—I
heard him say—he, Heriberto, who I knew knew just a little
history about Charles Olson—to all of Berkeley and to "the
whole system" and to that whole "co-opted" place on the one

day of torrential rain in May—I heard him say (and I agreed because I was always agreeing): "Frankly, my dear place, I don't want to build a dam." In this *our* authority lies.

And, you may ask, how do I know these facts, *how do I*, Carla, the letter b. (who in my imaginings could in fact BE my hero Heriberto Yépez, Hache, the letter "H"), know that Heriberto Yépez really knows very little history about Charles Olson and fakes his Oedipal critique of him as *a possible joke* on the repressed gringo readers who cover their asses? How do I know, here, from somewhere north and south of a border, with only a few dollars and the hermeneutic lessons I learned from a kind SoCal scholar? That will be the subject of my next epistle in which, sadly, I talk about Heriberto, how that young man I once knew was gone, how could it be said that his oeuvre had concluded before it began, / and how a little history and the promise of sex with consequences broke his links with me and my bond with him, my hero, Heriberto Yépez, Hache, and his theory of the empire of Charles Olson.

A Second Open Letter to North American Readers—re: how a little history and the promise of sex with consequences broke my bond with my hero, Heriberto Yépez, and his theory of the empire of Carlos Olson

by Carla, the letter b.

I know a man who knows just *un poquito de historia*. This man, *un hombre mysterioso*, put in question the bond with my prankster hero, Heriberto Yépez, (of whom I wrote you in my first letter) because this mysterious man's writings made me ask: What, exactly, was my relationship with Heriberto? What was it based on? Could I be satisfied with what the North Americans call *sex, lies, and videotape*—Heriberto wrote about some of these things—rather than the Truth, particularly if the *sex*, as Heriberto has it, was not worth it? I remem-

ber Heriberto—seeming to favor the monastic life—had once

written me, Carla, the letter b, who used to be the favored

Carlo b. Carlo to him, and whose letters fell like leaves from

the trans-gendered Q'abala Lemon Tree:

> …In theory-world writing and sex fulfill you.
>> In theory-world if I ask a girl if she wants to fuck with me, she says she needs to think about it.
>> And so we both think about sex and that's it.
>> In reality things work very differently. There sex some-times happens. And if sex happens, sometimes other things also happen, like kids, love, family, hate or orgasms. Sex has consequences. In theory-world there are no consequences / just hypothesis.

> (Yépez, *THE TRUE LENGTH OF NEO-EMOTIONALISM (A SHORT STORY)*)

Well, Heriberto was right: sex is certainly *not* worth it if there

will be children or love or family or hate—better to be in the-

ory-world, yes—but then again, and this is where I first began

to fear (and tremble) for what Heriberto demanded of me:

"I'm so young," I said, "I'm so horny, I like *men and not men,* or-

gasms. You know what, Heriberto: Better to be excited in the

real world. I—just call me *Carla or Carlo Danger*—will face the stiff consequences."

But I digress, and I will tell you of this other man, who taught me just a little history, who helped me understand what happens when an abyss is opened and we all fall in as if we thought we were filling up the space with *something* that stands for history, but does not. This *something*, sadly, happened to be the shortcomings of my hero, Heriberto—when writing on the North American poet, Charles Olson—and the facts Heriberto really got wrong about him, no joke, and how we tried to save him from his own theory of no consequence, and how another man who knew even *just a little history* could be so dangerous that we considered the nuclear option to make him vanish. But I digress.

Many years ago, hoping to meet Jorge Borges while on a happy holiday in Argentina, I met instead the Sephardic master of contemporary rabbinical exegesis, José Faur. Faur was in the same Jewish hermeneutic "business" as my own ancestor, the Egyptian French painter and Q'abala author Carlos Guisseppe Suarès who, in his commentaries, had deciphered the meanings of the biblical text *The Song of Songs* (yes, my sexual appetite had a scriptural lineage). There are lines in these Songs which unveil a desire for a Shulamite, whose "rounded thighs are like jewels." Yet my ancestor, Señor Suarès, realized that the Hebrew word for "jewels," *hhalaeem*, has at its root, *hlal,* "to writhe" so that, really, rabbinically and mystically, there was some dirty dancing going on here: Madonna's Q'abala with consequences, of course. When I saw that José and I had my ancestor and a bottle of Tequilla and some dancing girls and boys in common, I knew right then there would be orgasmic consequences.

One drunken night, I told José of my plans: to "translate" the keys to my ancestor's interpretive legacy into my own poetry—to be a critic and poet and editor and translator, in Spanish *and* in English, the going from one to the other which I still had to master. So he confessed to me this: "You need a master with a method in order to be a critic and a poet and editor and translator in Spanish and in English, so I will

guide you north. There is, in the works, in *Nueva York*, in
one Señor Árbol de Almendras' office, a blossoming English
translation of my hermeneutical text, *Golden Doves with Silver
Dots*. It sits with *el hombre* who is editing it— you should meet
this *hombre* (at least in print)."

Of course, I did not know at the time, but this man I was
to meet never received credit for his editing work. In fact, it
was only from José's Homeric rum-wet lips that I knew his
name, a Señor al-Quala whom I imagined going as blind as a
batty Borges telescoping and deciphering the dots and letters
of Jose's text in the damp, wine-dark offices of Señor Árbol de Almendras. This Señor al-Quala was a Sephardic Jew
whose family were refugees to America. He was a poet and a
scholar, from whom I could learn English and, perhaps, *just the
little history* Heriberto had forgotten.

My research drew me closer to Señor al-Quala. I discovered
he had a history of tracing the political and cultural footprints
of *al-andalus* in the contemporary Jewish and Arab worlds.

I uncovered his translations of the great Cuban Jewish poet, José Kozer. I learned that he was a poet and scholar who had corresponded with the legendary Spanish novelist, Juan Goytisolo, who had concluded that "the spirit of al-Quala's rigor and honesty" was in the tradition of "intellectuals free of mythical, exclusivist, nationalist or religious blinkers…." And I had heard that Señor al-Quala, too, desired a young Spanish/English editor and translator, like his own Señor Árbol de Almendras summoned him to redact José Faur's illuminated texts, and that this could be me, so I dreamt. If only our correspondence would lead to our meeting, so I might then trust in his teaching me to be a poet, a critic, an editor and translator who could learn, well, *just a little history*, although how could I know at the time—do I digress—how ironic and fateful it was that he, this Señor al-Quala, would lead me to a book of his still to be written, informed by years of his personal and poetic alliances with of all poets, Charles Olson, the very poet Heriberto, my hero, would also write upon. Thus, you see, as I foresaw, my dilemma: my "meeting" with Señor al-Quala's Olson would have

consequences—like sex—on my relationship with Heriberto's hypertextual Olson, which had its shortcomings. Sex with
two images of a 6'8" Olson! Who could imagine that I would
be in the middle and have to choose between them?

I want to say here, for my North American readers, because
I want to be as honest and clear as can be, that when I was
younger I admired Heriberto, I almost loved him, at least in
theory-world. Like his rage at Olson, I was what you call short
and angry at my father. I—just call me *Carla or Carlo Danger*—vented and mocked Norte-Americanos and played textual
dress-up and wrote "pink" lettristic make-up on my black pants
suits and trolled the post-ironic, cynical plots of the avant-
dead on the Tijuana and Oakland borders and I would, had
I been an actor with a clear target, the way Heriberto had la-
sered his endless monologue upon his bullseye Olson, well I
would have gone backstage blindfolded and picked up any prop
and wielded it as a club against "the man," any man, *el hombre,* Charles Olson, Walt Whitman, Octavio Paz, it didn't matter, maybe even harangue the blind, lame master Borges with

his own cane. *Carla or Carlo Danger* empathized with Heriberto's affairs and claims.

I was aligned with Heriberto's every anti-imperialistic, cynical, parodic move, even though I discovered he could, sometimes, be sincere. For example, the Black American innovative traditions of poetry, as he had written.

> Mexican writers understand poetic innovation and experimentalism in a way that resembles the self-understanding of black innovative tradition. As a culture fundamentally constructed to resist imperialism and alienation (and now globalization) we can't help but to be a counter-proposal to Western literature.

This, I thought, was no joke: he believed it. Two traditions: African-American and Latino—aligned in resistance: stickin it to the Western *hombre*. "I think," Heriberto wrote "we [Latin Americans] have more things in common with the African-American idea of innovations than with the 'white' one." Yes, I believed Heriberto, but with his self-confessed satirical nature one never knew his motives, which was fine, since he was funny, and I liked "funny," and I laughed. Like when I heard him say his clever truisms—ah, the profoundly ambivalent amoral pseudo-Nietzschean post-ironic nihilistic avant-

dead poses spoken in largesse—to an audience of graduate

students, among whom, I confess, I sat, hearing Heriberto:

> "families are artificial structures—it becomes an artificial sys-
> tem—it's a fake system"

> "the 'united states'—it's a fantasy"

> "Change is a 20th century myth. When I try to change the
> world, nothing happens—there's just more violence. Maybe
> Bush doesn't want to change. Maybe he's happy that way (au-
> dience laughs). I'm sure Bush is happy with his life. Why try to
> change someone who is happy (more laughter)?"

As I said, I like funny, even witty, but I also liked that Heri-

berto could be serious, particularly when he spoke of Afri-

can-American literary traditions. For example, in one essay,

he referenced poets whom I, too, had discovered to be earnest,

good poets—Harryette Mullen and Lorenzo Thomas and so

on—that, I thought, well, he means it, he respects these writers,

their innovative traditions. He's not joking.

Yet I dug deeper. I asked: where, in Heriberto's citings, was probably the most famous of the innovators in this pantheon of contemporary African-American writers, the revolutionary poet, LeRoi Jones/Amiri Baraka: the one figure the other poets whom Heriberto cited would honor, who Lorenzo Thomas himself would see, along with John Ashbery, as "the most influential American poet—in terms of style—of the last quarter of the 20th century." I decided to find out for myself what was up with Heriberto's omission. I gathered a little history on my own, what the Greeks called *istorin*, as to where, if at all, Señor Baraka was in Heriberto's world-view.

I found he was nowhere. And this was odd, considering Heriberto was a so-called scholar of Olson, of whom none other than this Amiri Baraka once said, referring to contemporary poets, "well, Charles basically gave us all the canvas." Baraka, who once said Olson called for "a poetry that used history and place as an engine to wrest meaning from the present. To see how now got to be now and where was it going and where had it been." And I wondered: in Herberto's imaginings, why had Olson's *barca* de Empire sailed without any departing words from Señor Baraka?

I had learned from Señor al-Quala that there was a legacy, a chain of poets, from one generation to the next, who offered us revelatory occluded histories, an interpenetration of traditions, the reading and re-reading of wildly dissonant texts in relation to each other and the news of the universe. Personally, I could locate this in my own history: my ancestor Carlo Suarès was a master of unlocking the cipher codes in the physical sciences or the plurality of universes in hieroglyphs. Señor al-Quala had seen this, had brought these traditions into the light. I saw in his text a reference to a film by one Mr. Ferrini in which Mr. Baraka spoke of the significance of Charles Olson and, yes, as one of the people whose concerns were often ignored, I was moved to tears:

> To me, Olson's concept of the polis was just simply the idea that you had to be grounded in the concerns of the people, that the people are finally the makers of history, and that you have to be grounded in what is historical in that sense. What are the concerns of the people? Why are they these concerns? The whole question of putting the hinge back on the door. That is, trying to find out what had been hidden from us by the emergence of this new one-sided society. That was important, particularly for me being black because I knew part of that was the connection to Africa. Where are the foundations of the world from? Charles was saying, "you have to go back, you have to go back."

I researched further. I found in al-Quala's book another extraordinary poet, Nathaniel Mackey, who had recalled that Olson himself knew and said in 1965 that he was "the White Man; that famous thing, the White Man, the ultimate paleface, the noncorruptible, the Good, the thing that runs this country, or that *is* this country. And, thank god, the only advantage I have is that I didn't...." Run the country, that is. Why? Because, as Mackey knew, Olson was almost alone among poets who "acknowledges"

> ... himself to be an heir to the corrupt power he condemns. He can own up to certain spoils the poet gathers from the workings of that power, can admit, as we have seen, that imperialism gives "a language the international power / poets take advantage of." In this we see the workings of not a clean but a troubled conscience.

> Olson sometimes speaks of political power as something from which he is excluded, promoting a sense of a priori exclusion as a way of confirming his poetic vocation. But there is another side of his thought that admits that for a white male poet like himself, born in a white-supremacist, male-supremacist society, political power, relatively speaking, is a birthright from which he isn't excluded but about which he has to make a choice. A man who was once on the threshold of a political career, as he was in the 1940s, more believably speaks of renunciation than of exclusion. That is exactly what we find him doing, exhorting others to choose "to be these things instead of Kings." For him poetry is analogous to a vow of poverty, a moral act of renunciation, as he writes very early in *The Maximus Poems*:

In the land of plenty, have

nothing to do with it

   take the way of

the lowest,

including

your legs, go

contrary, go

sing

And after reading in Señor al-Quala's book these words

of Mr. Baraka and Mr. Mackey, two of America's seminal po-

ets here honoring and quoting the legacy of Charles Olson, I

wondered, and I asked as if I were *saddened* by the whole affair:

why did Heriberto not know this history, given, as he *said*, his

bonds and correspondences with the African-American inno-

vative traditions? Now, in secret, I started having the strangest

thought—no, it was an uncanny dream—resembling how

my ancestor had dreamt his hermeneutics: no longer would

my ambition be to edit and translate Señor al-Quala, since a

different urgency dawned on me: I needed to become desperate enough to save Heriberto from embarrassing himself with his text on Olson, so much so that I wondered: was there still time to edit his *Empire of Neomemory,* post its English publication for readers whom he had attracted in the post-avant-garde, to save him from his own errors, from attacks by others, if not in the real world then maybe in theory world. I dreamt, as one option, hijacking police helicopters to circle Oakland and Tijuana and unloading confetti of errata slips. I dreamt there could be other, more fateful options—only to save Heriberto from himself.

Here, then, in Señor al-Quala's book, were a set of facts about the person of Olson and his poetry and his relationships that could have shamed Heriberto's theoretical admirers, had these facts about Olson been revealed. Yet how come no one knew this book (easy to understand why *Heriberto's* country-men would be in the dark about this text in American English, but how account for the Norte-Americanos' visions in their tunnels)? *Es mysterioso.* I wondered: How had Heriberto done it? How had he filled this/his Olson's poetic honey head with ideal, imperial fantasies and how did everyone fall in line and say "Amen we believe that is Charles Olson's head on the stake we always thought he hung from" as if they thought Heriberto were filling up the Olson space with *something* that stood for history, but was not? No doubt, I admired Heriberto's conviction and ambition, but I was confused—because it was not history or memory but theory. I should have realized it, since Heriberto had identified "Memory and History" together: "Memory is chimera….Memory and History are identical. They are the very impossibility of control."

And I wondered: if, as Heriberto had claimed, theory world was all there was, then where was there room for memory, particularly if memory was chimera? Although it pains me to put it like this—*because Heriberto could be clever and funny and like a true poet do-shaman tricks with beautiful, even compassionate words traversing all logic*—I was astonished: *because, in the context and consequences of people's real lives, that would make theory like revisionist history to survivors of genocide.* How could there possibly be space for what Señor al-Quala had written was the "solidarity [which] remains in *the integrity* of memory, as activities and meanings become codified for general consumption?" What strange meanings around Olson and empire had Heriberto codified for general consumption, and why?

Perhaps, as Señor al-Quala had written and Heriberto and his fans thought, it was easier to deal with Olson as…a "poet [who] comes to represent the inherited weight of patriarchy or is made out to be the priest-shaman-leader of a cult" [in the same, contemporary way, Señor al-Quala had said, "poets" are relegated to the "non-thinking" creative departments in the academy]. Perhaps it was easier to use his character, as Heriberto had done, "as a microanalogy for decoding the psychopoetics of Empire," ignoring reality in favor of an agenda. I wanted to save him from the dishonor that was about to be brought on us with Señor al-Quala's book.

And it must be understood: these were not only facts about Olson which one could look at and say, "well, look, Señor al-Quala has his facts and Heriberto has his facts and everyone has a different perspective" because Heriberto's facts really only did exist in theory world, as if he shared the stage with astronomers and was allowed to say yes "the moon is made of green cheese" or he proudly rose at a conference among African-American historians and then turned to his notes and said yes "Plantations were big open whitewashed places like heaven, and everybody on 'em was grooved to be there. Just strummin' and hummin' all day," as the young African-American Clay sarcastically said to his white female nemesis Lula in *Dutchman*, LeRoi Jones's/Amiri Baraka's 1964 play. So the shame to be avoided would be this: would the "*mexperimentalists*" (as Heriberto called them) and the avant-garde or post-avant *Norte-Americanos* be complicit in revisionist history: would they be complicit in a position difficult to defend with recourse to the mantra—"everyone has a right to his ideas with which we may not agree." Yet this is exactly what Heriberto's translators—well-intentioned and more than competent—wrote in their "Notes" at the end of *The Empire of Neomemory*: "Translation: we recognize that in writing as a collaboratively jumbled 'we,' each of us at different moments may end up seeming *to advocate ideas with which we do not agree.* (my emphasis) Translation: to sustain such discomforts. Translation: because we are dying inside this Empire." A fantasy panatopia of empire which Heriberto says Charles Olson's writing represented—meaning, we are all dying inside the body of Charles Olson's work. How do we get out from under his yoke? No joke.

Yes, I was anti-American and counter-conquest and wanted to believe Heriberto when he said the "United States" was "fantasy," or "'America' was a comical nightmare," because we all believed we were dying inside Empire and needed to breathe and we were seduced by Heriberto's idea that Charles Olson could be implicated in Fascism and the perpetuation of American Empire.

But, no matter how much it pained me, it was hard to believe Heriberto when I heard and saw otherwise: Here is what I heard and saw otherwise. In "This is Yeats Speaking," Carlos Olson had called Norte-Americanos on their own blindnesses in trying the fascist Pound for treason. Understanding just *a little history*, Señor al-Quala had witnessed an Olson who was implicated in just the *opposite* of what Heriberto had claimed: an Olson who called to the carpet the United States government's accommodation to Fascism, a government which would use the Pound trial to

> establish the shadowy image of the poet through whom art's relationship to politics can be administered and cordoned off, and used as a surrogate form of debate, like a condom placed over organs of policy and their effects.

Senor al-Quala remembered Olson's words in "This is Yeats Speaking":

> *What constitutes "our" side is not easy to see or state: to go no further than the term "democracy," left or center, it is too lazy, too dead of the past to include the gains of the present and advances to come. But the enemy, because he attacks, stands clear. A "fascist" is still a definition....*
>
> *We have not yet shaped, because we have denied this civil war, a justice with sanctions, strong and deep enough to measure the crime. Our own case remains unexamined. How then shall we try men who have examined us more than we have ourselves? They know what they fight against. We do not yet know what we fight for....*

And Señor al-Quala asked, why were the details of United States sponsorship of and links with fascist activities after the War something *which Olson alone, among the poets,* uncovered? "Our own case remains unexamined," Olson wrote, his knowledge of the "deep politics" involved a result no doubt of his position in The Office of War Information's Foreign Language Section, from which he resigned. Of these "deep politics," Señor al-Quala had written (and Heriberto forgot, no doubt, to say):

> Such "deep politics," in the sense poet and historian
> Peter Dale Scott has defined them in *Deep Politics and the*
> *Death of JFK*, get left by the wayside again and again, especially
> in trying to think through the relation of politics to
> history and culture. While all these Nazis were being
> brought into the government, Pound, a poet, was indicted
> in 1945, taken from Italy, and imprisoned in the District of
> Columbia Jail in Washington…. Never a real trial, the
> Pound case played an important cultural, historical, and
> political role. It established the shadowy image of the poet
> through whom art's relationship to politics can be administered
> and cordoned off, and used as a surrogate form of
> debate, like a condom placed over organs of policy and their
> effects. As mechanisms get jump-started by events, a series
> of stand-ins takes up the space of the actual, making it difficult,
> if not impossible, to talk about things outside their categorical
> function.
>
> The case of Olson, and his concern with "putting the
> hinge back on the door" to the past, follows a similar course.

Through Señor al-Quala, I now noticed an irony: had Heriberto, whom I admired and who loved theory world, used Olson as "a surrogate form of debate" for an America deeply involved in the workings of empire? Had he taken the same approach with Olson which American officials took with Pound? Had he just picked on the wrong guy and used him as one "in a series of stand-ins" for American empire? Had he used him as, *cómo sex dice en inglés*, his whipping cream boy (sic)? How could I save Heriberto from the facts as Olson and al-Qua-la had presented them in the real world, or was this even necessary since Heriberto only lived in theory world? I asked friends for advice, and they listened so closely that they came to me with their own dreams, like my American friend, Jeff (ah, the good *Godofredo*). He said he had heard talk of Heri-berto and his theories, how Heriberto thought Olson wanted "to flee from his real body" into "a replacement body," to live in language. Heriberto's vision of Olson's imaginary, theoretical co-bodies reminded him of a dream he had when in Mexico.

> I had a dream while in Mexico visiting my daughter when she was there studying Spanish. In the dream I was both me and Kafka, you know how you know that you are you but not you in a dream, yes?, and the not me who was me was Kafka. Anyway that is a minor point. The relevant moment in the dream was

when I or Kafk-I said to a friend walking along side me "Max [Horkheimer], theory is a cage in search of a bird...in this case, Big Bird." To which Max muttered something like "The complexity of the connection between the world of perception and the world of physics does not preclude...misguided theorizing. I'll buy the bird seed on the way home."

I laughed—I even thought Heriberto might find it funny, since, like me, he liked funny. I dreamt Heriberto had spilled big bird's seed, waiting for Olson to fly into his cage.

I dreamt my skin sweat and I was swarmed by cicadas and actually tried to read for the first time Charles Olson's poetry, very little of which, I now noticed as I was swatting the *psi psi* sounds of the persistent insects, Heriberto had remembered to cite in *The Empire of Neomemory*. Yes, I thought that the omission in a scholarly work of much of Olson's poetry was odd, although I was young and I respected the aging process and never wanted to fault someone for lapses of memory, *neo* or not. And, anyway, couldn't Heriberto be excused since he had already said that "memory [was] a provisional order," and "forgetting… a final substrate of the real?"

I found an Olson poem with the names of Leroy (sic) [Jones]

and Malcolm (X) in it: about fathers, immigrants, borders. It
went something like this:

> my father
> And I
> in the same land   like Pilgrims
> come to shore
> he paid
> with his life
> my father a Swedish
> wave of
> migration
> like Negroes
> now like Leroy and Malcolm
> X the final wave
> of wash upon this
> desperate
> ugly
> cruel
> Land this Nation
> which never
> lets anyone
> come to
> shore

The poem moved me. I felt for Charles Olson in the real world living in a nation which never let his father or anyone "come to shore." He was one of the great unwashed. I found a letter in which he said much the same to Ezra Pound:

> BUT you have to deal with us Olsons... your damn ancestors let us in (AND AS ABOVE I DON'T THINK THE BATH-TUB WAS SO CLEAN WHEN THEY DID). We're here. And to tell you your own truth you damn well know anglosax-onism is academicism and shrieking empire. LIFE out of Yale, CULTURE out of Princeton, and The BOMB out of Harvard.

Here was the Swedish Olson rejecting empire, seeing himself just like the gringos saw Heriberto and his people, a wave of unwashed wetbacks on the *frontera*, which made me wonder why Heriberto had made him the poetic front man for empire and had written that...

> Olson's verbal talent and his patriotic imaginary made him a perfect fit as an intellectual bureaucrat of the American propa-ganda machine....
> On the one hand, he continued to idealize the United States immigrant, an idealization he inherited from his father, and on the other hand his gift for nationalist rhetoric and his talents as a writer made him a key employee in the apparatus of petty propaganda. (Yépez, pg. 36)

...when I saw that he did not idealize anyone, at least not according to what he wrote in *The Post Office*:

[My father] valued America, as immigrants do, more than the native. I'm not sure it's a good thing. It wasn't, in my father's case, as this trouble he got himself into will show, though for me his fascination with the story of this country was fruitful, as it sometimes is, in the second generation American. There is a sentimentality about the freedoms of this country which none of the bitterness of poverty and abuse will shake in an immigrant. My father had it, at least up to this trouble I write about when the government of these States so failed him he was thrown back on that other rock of the immigrant, his foreign nationality organizations.

I discovered Olson was not Heriberto's nationalist naïf romanticizing the immigrant. He actually rejected both the government of the United States (the so-called rights it bestows on a citizen, which his father lost) *and* the immigrant societies which act as cocoons and into which an immigrant is tempted to withdraw when he gets rejected by his adopted country. He imagined that, had his father lived, and with the help of Gloucester, his local community, the *polis*, "he might have seen his 'struggle' *outside* both Sweden and America," outside the lines both demarcated. I wondered: how much did he sound like Heriberto at the *frontera:*

At the *frontera*, the Other is repelled. Both sides of the *línea* are rejected like two magnets of the same sign which only force could keep together, in so far as as soon as we allow them to operate according to their own rules, the separation is violent […] If the apparent theme is bidirectionality or symbiosis, the deeper theme, in contrast, is incompatibility"

(Heriberto Yépez, "La hibridación es un engaño. El significado real del arte fronterizo," *Made in Tijuana*, 2005).

Yes, "the deeper theme… [was] incompatibility," Heriberto wrote, and he was right and thus, ironically, resembled Olson, "the patriarch," the ancestor, the son of an immigrant father who had foreseen someone like Heriberto waiting on both sides of the *línea*, whose struggle could not harmonize the *"happy hybrid"*— Sweden and America. I was in a dilemma. I noticed that Heriberto was more like Olson than I thought, than even he thought. I remembered my friend, the mountain mystic, Juan Hirsch Luria, saying: "Well, Heriberto claims he is not interested in Charles Olson, but the fact is he's *possessed* by Olson—Are you joking me, he *fawns* and *fantasizes* over him. He wants to breathe through and kill daddy poet at the same time. It's what keeps him *alive*. 'The energy transferred from where [Heriberto] got it,' from the poet Charles Olson, to himself. It's what I call for Heriberto the return of the repressed or, in his case, projective verse!" And it was

already clear, given what Juan had said, that Heriberto was
so obsessed by "his father" that he wanted to keep him alive
by projecting his presence onto his own. I dreamt Heriberto
starring as Ray Milland helplessly screaming *Estoy Vivo! Es-*
toy Vivo! in Tijuana's film version of Poe's "The Premature
Burial." I dreamt trying to pry him from his self-made coffin.
And I remembered the night Juan had secretly whispered to
me how the seductive, crazy logical leaps and sinuous syntax
of Heriberto's language felt as if it aspired to the breath of Olson's prose, but I could not tell. Regardless, it did not make my
dilemma any easier. I wanted to breathe for my hero, Heriberto,
who could not breathe for himself.

Here was the dilemma, which cut three ways—it pained me to
say—as failed homage, parody, scholarship. I knew, of course,
that Heriberto was a provocateur who could get cranky and
intimidating, but I wanted to please him. I wanted to save him
from the real world from which he had deported himself. He
was, after all, the philosophical poster boy *por nihilismo* among
the young. So I wondered: first, if he was so much possessed by

the father, Olson, to mimic him, to fantasize over him, then how keep this homage a secret from his fans, who had, through Heriberto, savored their retribution on the master. Obviously, his so-called dismantling of Olson was a front and not very persuasive, particularly if I, with minimal training at the hip bone of a kind SoCal scholar, could see through the disguise and figure out he actually loved the master of empire, Mayan or otherwise. I give credit where credit is due: this interpretation of mine was revealed with Juan's help and a little bedtime reading of *Herr* Dr. Freud's Hamlet: "*mein Sohn* (*mi hijo*, my son), you only tear down what you can't stand (next to)."

Second, I had already determined, in my first letter, that this was no calculated fiction to deceive *Norte-Americanos*. My dilemma was how to conceal my disappointment in what brought me to Heriberto in the first place: his prankster-ism. It was clear his book on Olson did not reach the standards of Yepezian critical satire or what he named *crítica-ficción* (I articulated this in my first letter), particularly since I, again someone with not much hermeneutic practice, could see right through it, even before the scholars who had defended it as "serious scholarship."

Finally, and this greatly saddened me about how far my hero, Heriberto, had fallen, *The Empire of Neomemory* was now perceived as failed scholarship, theoretical over-determinism, revisionist history from an oedipally challenged grandstanding *nihilismo*, and it was being defended "up north" as "the view from Mexico," which hurt me because it absorbed his people in this whole affair and which I, after discovering from Mr. al-Quala's *a little history*, had to confront. I heard the oppositional, threatening bloggers, one in particular, a follower no doubt ensconced in Mr. al-Quala's anti-academicized cells, directly addressing Heriberto:

> Heriberto, if you believe "the post of Olson is evasion, the evasion of the history of the imperialist civilization to which he belonged," then the post of you, Heriberto, is *invasion*, the invasion of the academy of the avant dead civilization to which *you* belong. *Hoy usted* will be hoisted by your own petard.

The logic was so tight in its conviction that I imagined, in my loyalty to Heriberto, ways to silence Mr. al-Quala and his crew, to tighten the screws on them, who knew much through *a little history*. Ironically, Mr. al-Quala was *the mystery* man who would lead the life of me, Carla, the letter b., or Carlo Danger, or at least the life I had really wanted to live, since to everyone he would meet he would stay a stranger. He had hordes scoping him, but it didn't matter—he tried to fly under the radar. Still, the young North-Americans avant and post-avant-garde(rs) had to take a stand. They had been seduced by the disarming elegance of Heriberto's language, by the lispy playfulness of his Plathian ethos—Daddy, Daddy, you basard (*sic*0), I'm through—by the anti-Norte-American0 pose of this *hombre* from Tijuana, a literary province, mind you, certainly not the capital of Mexican letters—who was going after the imperial posse from Up North. It was clear the al-Quala posse had to be stopped. A little history had taught me that the only way anything would be settled was that some-one had to vanish, and why not Mr. al-Quala.

The set-up, in theory, was perfect: Yes, it was true, forces were at work to belittle Heriberto, but they were not imperial forces.

Instead, they were as anti-American as he, but in reality not theory. One of these was Mr. al-Quala, who had a little bit of a shadowy history himself. He knew much, too much. More than that: he remembered too much, and the few people behind him remembered what he said, even in an age when "memory was chimera." In the past, and in reality, he had been the target of a North American Academic Campus Watch. He appeared on lists of dangerous tenured professors who were framed as anti-American, pro-Palestine, anti-Israel in an article straight out of the government's vigilance handbook, a piece entitled, "Poetry, Terror, and Political Narcissism." If he were scoped, I thought, it would be the campus conservative watchdogs who would be suspect. No one would look our way.

Further, because we all knew that for Heriberto "memory is chimera," and "memory and history are identical," Señor al-Quala was what Heriberto hated most, an archivist of knowledge, whose work remembered—no found—what had been lost, no doubt like Olson's. I'm sure that, according to Heriberto, his work, like Olson's, was "an

expansion towards the other, towards the fusion with an appro-
priation of the other....Olson [who] devours the other, [who]
swallows the other into his own life, and likewise, is devoured
by his prey...." For Olson, Heriberto had said, "erudition is
a hoarding, defined by banking and expedition" and, thus,
empire. And so, Señor al-Quala was implicated as well. And
since Señor al-Quala was already suspect, I wondered, most-
ly because of my loyalty to Heriberto who taught me the
meaning of irony and renunciation of change in a post-Mexican era void of truth, did my Heriberto devotees and country-
men and young Norte-Americano avant-garde(rs) have access
to stockpiles of whatever the post-avant nuclear option might
be in order to make Señor al-Quala and his cells and their
kind of "little history" disappear, not in theory but in fact.
(We imagined stockpiles of disappearing inkwells mushroom-
ing in a blogged down age which welcomed hyper-tolerant
equivalents of flat earth theory?) What if he and his writings
were "disappeared," lost, never to be found? The only question
remaining: would it be fission or fusion? Heriberto, I knew,
would have favored fission. For Heriberto's sake, there would

be no dialogue with history, no false coherences, no textual fusion of cultures, which for Heribeto meant "fascist remix." For Heriberto, there would only be fission unleashed in one lit quaked city by the Bay.

But it was not an option, practically or theoretically, and the thought vanished as soon as it was triggered. The problem was deeper, since Heriberto's writing would still be present for any future avant-garde(r) to unearth. In the end, my dilemma came down to this: The Heriberto I loved had become a disappointing fraud, at least in terms of his knowledge of Olson, but the fact was I loved him precisely because he had always been a disappointing fraud. He acted the literary roles expected of him, as Mexican critic, or so he said, "performing a kind of role-playing as an author within a specific culture (in this case, the Mexican Republic of Letters)." He wanted, he said, to build "communication between our two cultures through imaginary entities and lies." His "fictive criticism…was part of a *diálogo diablo* (to use Groussac's image) on the periphery of Latin America, a *devilish dialogue* or *diabolical dialogue*, a sort of wanna-be experimental cross-cultural setup which [could] accomplish much more than more serious academic approaches." He was, to an extent, a little like me, when I worked for that kind SoCal scholar, when I hoped my skills would gain me entry into a dialogue with her on the heroes and anti-heroes of literature. For example, I would have treasured, like the recovery of a trunk full of manuscripts, a dialogue with her about my other hero, my distant cousin, Carlos Bernardo Soares, who once said:

> I am the sort of person who is always on the fringe of what he belongs to….. Everything around me is evaporating. My whole life, my memories, my imagination and its contents, my personality—it's all evaporating. I continuously feel that I was someone else, that I felt something else, that I thought something else. What I'm attending here is a show with another set. And the show I'm attending is myself.

Hearing my cousin, distant though he was, it hit me: my bond with Heriberto had always been as a person on the fringe of what I belonged to—since there was really nothing there with me and Heriberto, except in theory, as there was really nothing there with Heriberto and Carlos Olson, except in theory. Curiously, perhaps this was the way Heriberto would have wanted things to end: to be represented by a fact-less biography that explained nothing. So be it. Let him rest, resign, not be, be himself. He had tried to be authoritative and I had tried to save his image, but something else had to happen to rescue him from his "post-Mexican" identity. Maybe he had to become post-Heribertoan.

In fact, one could even say that in my separating from Heriberto, my hero, he had actually succeeded, because I came along to free him from his scholarly follies in order "to destroy his authority as a critic" (these were Heriberto's words, not mine), which he never liked, or to save him from creating yet another irony to hide his vulnerability in the real world… (I never did that, people heard me confess I almost loved him). But if only a little history was what it took for the memory of Heriberto to be, well, chimera, then, so be it, our bond would have to be broken. Yes, of course I was saddened that it had all come down to a vanishing act in order to break my bond, that it all had to go up in smoke, so to speak. But what else could I do but let him go? As he once wrote, and as every one of us knew, "all this role-playing was utterly nihilistic and boring." And certainly my loyalty to Heriberto, no matter my disappointments, would not allow someone else to just come along willy-nilly and use his irony against him, which is why, plain and simple and not in theory, he had to go before anyone came back for vengeance, lest some stranger come along one day and say with pleasure

"Heriberto, hoy, usted will be hoisted by your own petard."

AFTERWORD

by Benjamin Hollander

It is an irony not lost on me that the publisher of the extraor-
dinary Chax Press, Charles Alexander—or Charles, the letter
A.—has entrusted me to offer an afterword on these strange
Letters of Carla, the letter b. (which as a phrase or title seems
to make no sense) and, before her, the words of The Future
Guardian of the Letters.

I feel as if I don't belong here, like some rude interloper between publisher and authors, and that I have no business being
in their business. Further, I feel that if I were, as it were, to get
involved, or were I to be, that is, beseeched to give my word,
well, then somehow I would be implicated in the whole affair
and readers would look back at me as being central to it rather
than an afterthought. In my own mind, I am an afterthought,
as attested to by this afterword, which is not an easy way to go

through life, if, that is, it could be called a life (although I do tend to have the final say, which is some small consolation). But apparently Charles has no such concern and has chosen me to be a no doubt Johnny come lately interlocutor of sorts, perhaps to project some objective critical *stance towards reality* on this whole affair. This reality can be as Stevens wrote, "an Activity of the Most August Imagination" (and in reality and by coincidence my birth date is August 26), able to create correspondences, transformations…

> The visible transformations of summer night,
> An argentine abstraction approaching from
>
>> And suddenly denying itself away
>> There was an insolid billowing of the solid
>> Night's moonlight lake was neither water nor air.

…which may have happened under the same moonlight which George Oppen openly wonders about and cannot name when he looks out with his wife, Mary, when that light in his poem, "The Forms of Love," changes almost by caprice into mist by the evanescent pronoun "it":

We groped
Our way together
Downhill in the bright
Incredible light

Beginning to wonder
Whether it could be lake
Or fog
We saw, our heads
Ringing under the stars we walked
To where it would have wet our feet
Had it been water

But enough about "it."

As I said, Charles has his reasons for choosing me to have

the last word. He knows I have a little history with letters: as

co-editor of *A Book of Correspondences for Jack Spicer,* as well

as *Letters for Charles Olson.* More to the point, or to the letter,

Charles himself has published my syllabically fractured work—

his fine, letterpress edition of my *Levinas and the Police*—and

knows of the Kabbalistic permutations imprinted in my poems

in *The Book Of Who Are Was.* Further, he is aware of my work

as editor of essays on Paul Celan's translations, as well as my

critical writings, so all in all it would make sense he would ask

for a brief exegesis on these letters and would consider me to be "the man for the job." Finally, no doubt Charles has deduced and posed this question: since there was a mention by The Future Guardian of the Letters of a Tribe of John Ashbery, could a Tribe of Ben be far behind? Thus, like Ben Jonson, could there be the possibility of my running with my own band of merry-men, there being a gang I could consult even if I myself had no opinion on the words there-in nor even a gang in tow, **Il Gruppo** aside, to consult? But enough about me.

The text quite literally before me for commentary is as much a puzzle to me as it must be to you, dear reader, whether represented by Carla, the letter b., or by the future guardian of what I assume are her letters. In other words, I'm with The Lovin' Spoonful here: "she's still a mystery to me."

As such, where I should offer closure, I only have questions. For example, was The Future Guardian of the Letters on the level? Or was he, as the expression goes, half a bubble off plumb? Further, was he master of the turn around and double speak? I say this because, when listening to him, I find it difficult to trust him. Would not any hermeneutic reading of these texts, for instance, be skeptical of the intentions of a guardian who exposes an author whose "forswearing" at one and the same time says "I give up, no more of me," and then all but commits perjury by being unable to stop speaking? And then, absurdly, the guardian follows suit, promising even more testimony from the characters and the plot he forwards. Personally, I would want the author and the guardian to be true to their words—to protect and to serve being their highest priority—and then just shut up and burrow into the background. But that's just me.

Alas, that is not the case, and I am left to wonder—where is all this going? How can my afterword interpret this whole affair? I think I have a clue….which may clarify the mystery in poetry before me.

The mystery begins with the end of the book of letters. What I mean is that what happens at the end of both the text of the future guardian and the texts of Carla the letter b. gives me an

opening I can interpret, where the subject of one is the predicament of the other, where the one called The Future Guardian
of the Letters must vanish in order to open a space for the other, Carla, to speak, and who, at the end of her letter must also
vanish or, in her case, speak of leaving or, more to the point, or
to the letter, has to let her hero, Heriberto, go, so must leave
to save him. *So what we have here are texts of leave taking, each
saving and staking a path for the next one. But why—to what end?
Who needs to walk in here? What is the point?*

What if the point is to open yet another door for a shadow
heteronym to enter, or, to be less dramatic, a writer who will
open the future of this book even further, but this time as a
comrade, a once long ago enemy within the world of identity
politics who could be an ally to the future guardian, to Carla, to
Carlos, and, perhaps, even to the forsworn author and his heirs?
Could the body of this someone even be, in the turn-around of
turn-arounds, one of the bones of contention in these letters,
say, one Señor Heriberto Yépez (although his name in the end
does not matter, it is the creator who withdraws himself who

matters)? But why would I assume he is, like I am to Charles, "the man for the job of a friend indeed?" Why would I conclude that he, or someone in his stead, would be the one who needs to speak, at some point, in order to reconcile and make amends with all the characters here?

Well, if I try to read his writing and if I follow the clues laid down by the others before this afterword, I can see his character has prefigured as much. For one thing, I can't find much work of his online. Why, dear reader, should this fact—the presence and absence of his (or any) writing—matter?

Well, for one thing, I could read his hiding as shyness, as introspection, as a potential act of benevolence and openness. Think of it as the classic shell game: when his work disappears in one incarnation, it reappears as another, which has covered up his forebear. Seriously, this is insane, beautifully insane. When people ask for a virtual link to this guy, well, there's no URL....He has made it his job to vanish his writing. And, ironically, he has done it in an age (so unlike the one the future guardian says he comes from) when everything there is is supposed to be there to link to and see so that the discussion boards do anything *but* collapse. His blogs are emptied—like trash—older "posts" on poetry become invisible in English or turn into Spanish or turn no more or turn to mush and then are gone. Anon. He uses the internet against itself, he takes things down. For good. And it is good. Instead of spreading the news far and wide, instead of serving the many not the one, he seems to want to hide inside the internet. To lie dormant. And it is good.

It is he who is the lapsed figure of the virtual church. On the one hand, his writings go up online and then come down, and, on the other, when they do come down and cannot be recovered and reached by virtue of the Wi-Fi, they open the possibility not only for the future of a book to be re-written in print but for the future of the many enemy authors and their stand ins as, of all things, potential friends to come in unscripted, like Heriberto himself, as if the book were an open theatre, for him to appear and disappear with his pseudonymous writing projects, his *crítica-ficción*, his fading in and out and so on....

And—to get to the point—rather than see him, as some did (for example, the irritable people of Il Gruppo), as the villainous cynical persecutor of Olson-hood, there is a chance to see him—and, more importantly, the idea of him—as one of the Goodfellows—evidence for this possibility is in the text of the forsworn author's *apologia* where he says "he was not that jerk or witless"—one of whose writings, if and where they can be found, I (and even Il Gruppo) might even agree with.

For example, take his condemnation of what he rightly calls "the police art" of the conceptual poets—the names Kenneth Goldsmith and Vanessa Place—so right on target—or his critique of the Berkeley Conference of 2015 (*Crosstalk, Color, Composition*), so right on target, both commentaries still accessible through other people's websites, in which he wonders why, in the words of the organizers, they emphasized inviting

> poets of color of **national reputation**....with "the goal of the conference's design [being]to enlarge **national paradigms for reading and writing poetry** by creating a space in which poets of color may define the issues central to their poetry and imagination.

Why, he asks—and I would ask likewise—is the focus "on the National, the National, the National?"

> What the national element is doing is warding off the foreign, the alien, the unwelcomed, the transnational…. By making it a national-colored conference, the participants were structurally invited to remain within the confines of the nation state of poetics, that is, the color element (which is historically foreign) became tamed, weakened, controlled. This is what the element of "composition" also emphasizes: color was asked to compose itself according to the nationalistic….Nationhood became a formula to ensure civility.

This is exactly right. He makes perfect sense: that this, often blind to itself "national" consciousness "warding off the alien" is the elephant in the room of the most supposedly forward-looking , avant-garde poetry communities, and it has been Jumbo for a long time. Its history goes back, in its most recent iteration, to the language poets, one of whom he has edited in the first Spanish prose anthology of this poet's work (let the irony not be lost on Señor Yépez). It is a history which can be seen in the original issues of L=A=N=G=U=A=G=E magazine, from 1978-81: the relative indifference towards "the foreign"—the parochial and monolingual perspectives on poetry—evidenced by the exclusion of acts of translation or writing on translation or by poets outside North America and "the West" in general. That's what a little history tells us. It seems any so-called progressive poetics can be accepted as long as no one has to work to learn a language other than the one into which they were born.

So this is where we are alike, where we agree, as if we were to pronounce: no more walls, no more poet-like addresses, let's walk together, me and Heriberto, Carla, the letter b. and *Hache*, the letter H, or the forsworn author and the editor and Guillermo, off we go, as pals, and so what, no big deal, if "here is another fine mess we've all gotten ourselves into." Did not he (Yépez) say the journey would be plural? Did he not suggest with The Future Guardian of the Letters that poetry could mean any possibility in writing for the imagination to *be* anonymous and multiple and free?

> Understanding 'writing' as an open process of reinventing its identity, and understanding 'identity' in general not as a fixed list of attributes of something/something, but *identity* as a *series of patterns and methods of changing one-another.* (Yépez)
>
> Poetry then means the new-making of oneself. (Yépez)

So by "poetry" I-I just don't mean "verse" but the *construction (poiesis) of oneself.* (Yépez)

And, as such, as inevitable, the deconstruction of oneself. To be joined in this venture by another, by others.... "In the plural. Should we not want "to learn how to liberate oneself from hegemonic 'one'*self* constructs." Everything he did pointed to this act of liberation. And so everything he did pointed to the others in this drama which composed *The Letters of Carla, the letter b. and* their freedom, their return as the beings of The Book in waiting....

And was this not where the future guardian of the letters told us he lived, exactly, outside that virtual world, where almost all has vanished until the beings return where else but to the possibility of the book to be in print, yet again? As it should be. On its own. And that to truly be forsworn, any author—and this would include the guardian, the forsworn author himself, Carla the letter b. among all the others—would have to wait for the many—friends, indeed—to complete them (could that be Heriberto himself I see coming towards us) to continue them in the dormant-text with its invitation for guerrilla allied heteronymic egoless scriptors and their tactics, their weapons now laid on the ground, their book still to come, their final mystery being-asking:

> "Whose words will lie in wait to take over
> after there is no more of me?

Anon."

About the Author

Benjamin Hollander (1952-2016) lived for the past three decades in San Francisco, after moving there with his wife, Rosemary Manzo, in 1978. He taught English, Writing, and Critical Thinking, primarily at Chabot College, in Hayward. He passed away on November 21, 2016. He is the author of the following books:

Translating Tradition: Paul Celan in France
    (editor; ACTS, 1988)
How to Read, too (Leech Books, 1992)
The Book of Who Are Was (Sun and Moon, 1997)
Levinas and the Police, Part 1 (Chax Press, 2001)
Vigilance (Beyond Baroque, 2004)
Rituals of Truce and the Other Israeli (Parrhesia Press, 2004)
In the House Un-American (Clockroot Books, 2013)
Memoir American (Punctum Books, 2013)
Letters for Olson (editor; Spuyten Duyvil, 2016)

About Chax

Founded in 1984 in Tucson, Arizona, the mission of Chax is to create community through the publication of books of poetry and related literature that are works of integrity and vision, and through the presentation of poets and other artists in public programs as well as in dialogue with each other in symposia. Chax has published 200 books in a variety of formats, including hand printed letterpress books and chapbooks, hybrid digital and letterpress chapbooks, book arts editions, and trade paperback editions such as the book you are holding. In August 2014 Chax movied to Victoria, Texas, and is presently located in the University of Houston Victoria Center for the Arts.

Recent and in-progress books include *Lizard*, by Sarah Rosenthal, *Dark Ladies*, by Steve McCaffery, *Andalusia*, by Susan Thackrey, *Limerence & Lux*, by Saba Razvi, *Short Course*, by Ted Greenwald & Charles Bernstein, *Diesel Hand*, by Nico Vassilakis, *An Intermittent Music*, by Ted Pearson, *Arrive on Wave: Collected Poems*, by Gil Ott, *What We Do: Essays for Poets*, by Michael Gottlieb, *Autocinema,* by Gaspar Orozco, *any would be if,* by Norman Fischer, and several other books to come.

You may find CHAX online at *http://chax.org*